Aspects of the History of

Copper mining in Namaqualand 1846-1931

John M Smalberger

C. STRUIK (PTY) LTD.
CAPE TOWN JOHANNESBURG 1975

C. STRUIK (PTY) LIMITED
Africana Specialist and Publisher, 56 Wale Street, Cape Town

ISBN 0 86977 043 8

Designed by W. Reinders
Printed in South Africa by Citadel Press,
Polaris Road, Lansdowne, Cape

Contents

Acknowledgements

My interest in Namaqualand and its mines was first aroused by the lectures of Professor H. M. Robertson, Emeritus Professor of Economics at the University of Cape Town. It was at his suggestion that I undertook research into the subject. As sponsor and mentor of the thesis upon which this book is based his unfailing criticism and help were vital, and, without his constant assistance in innumerable ways, this book would never have been completed.

There are many other people to whom I am indebted. I would, however, like to express my sincere thanks to Miss Sellicks, formerly of the Library of Parliament, Miss Jooste and the late Miss Wahl, also of that institution, for unstinting aid in the course of research, to Andrew Purkis and Gretchen Smith who are mainly responsible for the table of copper prices and to the staff of the South African Library.

Last but not least, I should like to express the deep debt of gratitude I owe to Elizabeth van Heyningen, Marian George and Allan Isted who read parts of the typescript and corrected many errors.

List of illustrations

Introduction

The object in undertaking this work has been to present a picture of Namaqualand and its mines. This picture is by no means complete, but it is hoped that the pages which follow will in a small way contribute something to the history of Namaqualand.

The early explorations are described in the prologue. Not all the early travellers to Namaqualand have been mentioned, since not all have had anything of significance to add on the development of the copper mines. What we have attempted to show is that while Europeans learnt of the existence of copper in Namaqualand from the Namaquas shortly after the settlement of the Cape, the difficulties of transport prohibited the development of these mines.

The first chapter tells the story of The South African Mining Company. This company was the first mining concern to commence actual operations in Namaqualand and the first public mining company in South African history. For these reasons its development has been discussed in such detail.

The second chapter recalls the copper mining mania of the 1850s. All too often, the very existence of such a boom is forgotten. Its importance lies in the fact that, as the first purely speculative boom of any extent in the history of South Africa, it introduced South Africa to one of the typical features of a modern economy.

The question of leases is examined in the third chapter. Special attention is devoted to this because the final settlement of the lease question, involving the vesting in the State of mineral rights to the mission grounds, has been a factor contributing to the present situation existing at these stations. It is a matter of interest, but also of regret, that the development of Namaqualand's mineral wealth reflected in many ways to the detriment of the original inhabitants of the territory.

The fourth chapter deals with the rise and development of the most important mining areas in Namaqualand and with the problems of transport. Of necessity the material chosen must reflect the idiosyncrasies of the author – taking into account the period under review and the very scattered nature of the sources.

The epilogue brings the history up to date. The coverage once again is limited, this time excluding all discussion of social questions.

Prologue

Although the terms Copper Age, Bronze Age and Iron Age cannot be applied to the Namaqua and other Khoi,[1] we may state with certainty that the Namaqua knew and mined both copper and iron.[2] The first contact with the Namaqua was made at the southern border of their region by an expedition under the leadership of Pieter van Meerhof in 1661.[3] Van Meerhof was 'clearly surprized' by the wealth of metals displayed by the Namaqua:

> Their dress consists of all kinds of beautifully prepared skins...gorgeously ornamented with copper beads...Their locks they thread with copper beads, covering their heads all over. Around their necks they have chains, slung round them 15 or 16 times. Many have round copper plates suspended from these chains. On their arms they have chains of copper and iron beads which go round their bodies 30 or 40 times. Their legs are encased in plaited skins, ornamented with beads...Their only industry is working in copper and iron, from which they make very neat beads and chains.[4]

Further evidence was obtained in 1681 when a party of Namaqua were induced to visit the Castle and brought with them specimens of rich copper ore.[5] Following upon this, a certain Olof Bergh was sent out in 1682 and again in 1683 in search of the source of the copper ore – although both expeditions failed in their purpose. However, in February 1684, a second party of Namaquas visited the Cape. When they returned to their homeland Sergeant Isaq Schrijver with 15 soldiers and three miners were sent with them. The sergeant succeeded little better than Ensign Bergh, though he managed to penetrate somewhat farther into Namaqualand and to collect a number of pieces of copper ore, which he brought back on a pack ox, from the people he visited there. This ore was melted in crucibles and the pure metal was sent as a specimen to the directors.[6] Additional information must have been obtained, for in 1684 we find in the resolutions of the Council of Policy further mention of the copper deposits of Namaqualand. Apparently the copper mountain lay not far from the sea, where there was alleged to be a good harbour on the coast for small vessels. It was intended to send a small vessel to explore the coast, to survey the harbour, and to examine the intervening country to the 'Copper Mountain'.[7] It is not known however, whether this advice was acted upon. Presumably it was not, for one of the objects of Simon van der

Stel's expedition to Namaqualand was to find a suitable harbour.

The expedition led by van der Stel was an extremely imposing one consisting, as it did, of a party of 57 Whites, a Macassar prisoner of state Dane Mangale and his servant, and three Black servants of the Commander. One carriage with six horses, eight asses, 14 riding horses, two field-pieces, eight carts, seven wagons – one loaded with a boat, and 289 draught or pack oxen were included.[8] One of the members of the party was a mineralogist in the employ of the Company, a certain Frederich Mathias van Werlinckhof, who had been sent out as Chief Mining Engineer to be in charge of operations on the west coast of Sumatra but who was also to report on the minerals at the Cape on route.[9]

In van Werlinckhof's report on the Namaqualand copper fields he stated that he had at all times kept the Commander fully informed as to the nature of the rocks passed. As it was their primary aim to reach the copper mountains of which they had heard, not very much time was devoted to what appeared to be of only passing interest. On reaching the so-called 'Koperberg' they engaged in an active search for copper ore. The Commander, apparently with 'great zeal' and 'taking advantage of all the circumstances', investigated a part of the region intensively. Choosing the most promising spots, he launched the search for minerals. At one place, which was distinguished on the chart by the letters 'H.V.R.', they sank a shaft to a depth of three fathoms. Better and better ore was found the deeper they went. At this place, in fact, they found ore with pure metal disseminated through it. In van Werlinckhof's opinion it was '. . . certain and obvious that the deeper one goes the richer and richer the minerals will be'.[10]

Approximately a gunshot's distance away from this indication, another trial was made. This shaft was only taken down to a fathom and a half. It, too, proved to be a favourable spot. Copper and silver of similar quality to that found at the first trial was uncovered. This spot was designated 'S.M.'. Van Werlinckhof predicted that in working this trial, not only good minerals but possibly pure massive copper would be found. At about one or two gunshot's distance on the other side of the above 'mine', a third shaft was sunk. This was designated 'S.V.S.'. At this spot another trial to the depth of three els[11] was sunk. Van Werlinckhof concluded:

I am entirely convinced of the favourable character of these mines; in the event of mining operations being continued, richer and richer, and better minerals will be found, for the hills concerned extend several miles in length and breadth, and hold minerals almost everywhere, and in some places water for man and beast is plentiful, as the Commander found on personal inspection.[12]

These sanguine expectations of van Werlinckhof's did not, however, come to fruition.

Van der Stel forwarded some samples to the directors for testing. Three of these yielded from $7\frac{1}{2}\%$ to $11\frac{1}{2}\%$ of copper.[13] The deposits were thus very much poorer than had at first been thought, and considering the distance from markets unlikely to prove payable. As Theal expressed it:

...the steep declivities, the frightful ravines, the wastes of sand, and harbourless coast, were physical obstacles too great to be overcome.[14]

Although the existence of the Koperberg could now be indicated with certainty on maps of southern Africa, these deposits attracted only intermittent attention. The expedition is, however, important in many ways as pioneering contact between white and brown in the north-western part of the Cape. Thereafter hunters, livestock traders and others journeyed to the territory in increasing numbers, leading eventually to the rise of a landless, poverty-stricken, proletariat.[15]

In 1761 an expedition was once again despatched to Namaqualand, this time under the leadership of one Hendrik Hop. Included among this party was a burgher surgeon Dr Carel Christoffel Rykvoet who was to report on the mineralogy of the territory traversed by his group. Rykvoet, in his report which was published as an addendum to the *Nieuwste en Beknopte Beschrywing van de Kaap der Goede-Hoop* published by J. H. Schneider, Amsterdam, 1778, stated that he considered van der Stel's Koperberg poor, and that it contained only a small quantity of copper. Nevertheless, at a place very close by he found rich deposits and deemed that a mine could have been worked there had a sufficient quantity of wood and water been available. His highest praise, however, was reserved for certain deposits which lay close to the Orange River in the territory known today as the Richtersveld.[16] This ore was said by him to contain more than a third part of copper. Notwithstanding, he did not consider the working of these deposits an economic proposition, because of the hardness of the surrounding rock, an insufficiency of fuel for smelting the ore and the difficulties of transport. Ox-wagon transport would, he thought, prove prohibitive, while the Orange River because of its many reefs and shoals was not suitable for navigation.[17]

Once again the copper deposits of Namaqualand were largely ignored for an extended period of time, and while it has been asserted that Gordon and Paterson[18] actually commenced mining in 1780,[19] no proof of this can be found. It was not in fact until the expedition of James Alexander in 1836/37 that the existence of these deposits once again attracted any attention.

Alexander had originally intended to undertake an expedition to the eastern part of southern Africa, but being forestalled by Andrew Smith he decided upon an exploration of the western part of southern Africa. With the guidance of one Willem Josephs he was led to certain deposits of copper near the banks of the Orange River. The first specimen of ore obtained by him was forwarded to George Thompson of Cape Town, who handed it to Samuel Bennett, of the firm Bennett & Boulding. On Mr Bennett's return to England after an absence of 18 years spent in the Colony, he obtained the assay of Mr Johnson of Hatton Garden who certified that he found it to contain $27\frac{7}{8}\%$ of pure copper.[20] Bennett then approached General Napier, who had just received the appointment of Governor of the Colony, soliciting his encouragement and protection of any company that might be established for working the ore in question. Napier gave, as far as he felt able, every assurance that he would promote Bennett's interests should the occasion present itself. When it was learnt that Alexander was intending to return to England, the decision was taken in fairness to him to suspend the formation of the exploitation company until his arrival so that he could play a prominent part in the formation of any such company, as it would be based on his discoveries. Understandably it was hoped that he would be able to give more detailed information relative to his discoveries.[21] Alexander did go so far as to prepare a report but nothing more seems to have been done in the matter, although popular belief has it that Alexander actually did commence mining. This belief is probably based upon the vivid picture of events in Namaqualand at the time of this alleged activity drawn by Fred Cornell in his *The Glamour of Prospecting*. Despite his own admission that information on operations carried out some 70 odd years before was extremely difficult to find, Cornell went into some detail concerning these mining activities. Operations were abandoned, according to him, because of the strength of the prevailing winds which, in the days before steam navigation, prevented rapid handling of the ore.[22]

The missionary James Backhouse who visited Namaqualand in

the 1840s was less enthusiastic than Alexander about the prospects of working Namaqualand's mineral wealth. He considered that there was insufficient fuel to allow for large scale exploitation. In his *Narrative of a Visit to the Mauritius and South Africa*, published in 1844, he pointed out that:

In the latter country...(Namaqualand)...copper ore frequently occurs; it is so plentiful in some mountains which we passed that they are called Koperbergen, *Copper Mountains.* Probably it might be collected advantageously by the Namaqua Hottentots, and transmitted in their skin knapsacks, to some place on the coast where they might exchange it for other commodities; but to smelt it in this country would be impracticable. The only supply of wood that could be used for such a purpose is on the banks of the Orange River, and a few tributary streams, where the belt of wood is seldom twenty yards wide; from what I know of the quantity required, I think all that would be available for such a purpose would be consumed by a smelting-work in two to three years. The primitive nature of the whole country precludes the idea of the existence of coal; no coal is known in any part of South Africa except in the interior, at some distance from Port Natal. The only remaining article of fuel which could be obtained is cow-dung, and the quantity required would be too great to be supplied in a country capable of supporting so comparatively small a stock of cattle.[23]

Meanwhile Bennett's idea of forming a company to work the deposits discovered by Alexander took a more concrete form in 1843 with the publication of the *Outlines of a Prospectus to form a Cape of Hood Hope West Coast Trading and Mining Company*. In this it was noted that:

From the personal observation of Capt. Alexander in the region of the Copper Ore, and from Mr Bennett's suggestions, arising from so long an experience in that quarter and climate, it is ascertained that whether the Ores are to be brought to the mouth of the Orange River by oxen, mules or camels, by land, or by lighters down the Orange River, the result would be highly advantageous; but, as it is impossible to embark in a series of operations of so extensive a nature, without a preliminary survey and report by experienced persons, as to the faculties afforded by land or water, it is proposed that a fund be subscribed for obtaining so correct a Report, as may leave no uncertainty or doubt in future operations.

It is considered that the expense of such preliminary Survey cannot exceed £1 000 or £1 200, and the outlay will, in all probability, lead to advantages almost inexhaustible, as it is well known that the Country abounds in other species of Ores; and that the Wood to be cut down, to form a communication between the masses of Ore and the River, is of a most valuable character for furniture and other ornamental purposes.

It is proposed on the receipt of the Report, that the present Subscribers should meet together for the purpose of making arrangements for a Joint Stock Company, either on a limited or extended scale, as they may consider expedient.[24]

The Orange River Copper Company was only one of the projects put forward by The Cape of Good Hope West Coast Trading and Mining

Company. It was proposed that the latter concern should have a capital of £10 000 in 200 shares of £50 each, and was to be established under sanction of an Act of Parliament. Its objects were, firstly, to establish a port on the west coast (for which they considered Rooe-Wall Bay excellently situated); secondly, to establish The Orange River Copper Company; and lastly, to establish a number of trading centres. These outposts were to be protected by arms, following the example of the French traders. This undertaking apparently did not receive sufficient support for its establishment since nothing more was heard of it. As it had been suggested that the trading centres should also be missionary stations, the combination of philanthropic aims with military expenditure and investment in public works which would not bring in immediate returns to the promoters may have deterred potential investors. The attention that it drew to that remote corner of southern Africa was, however, directly responsible for stimulating the formation of The South African Mining Company in 1846. The latter concern may, in fact, be viewed as merely an extension of the former. The South African Mining Company was thus the first undertaking to commence mining in Namaqualand.

NOTES TO PROLOGUE

1 A. J. H. Goodwin: 'Metal Working among the early Hottentots', *South African Archeological Bulletin* 1956, p. 46

2 Goodwin claims that the Namaquas' knowledge of iron was derived from their intercourse with the BaTlaping. Ibid, p. 48

3 The Dutch East India Company was a commercial body. As such, it was anxious to carry on trade in a broad sense and also to discover the potential of the places where it had set up its flag. Whenever exploring parties were sent out from Cape Town their leaders were instructed to search for minerals and to note the physical features of the country. Between 1659 and 1664 there were six expeditions despatched into the interior in order to attempt the discovery of *vigiti magna*. For a short survey of these see Dr E. E. Mossop, *Old Cape Highways* (Cape Town, Maskew Miller nd). For the journals kept on these expeditions reference should be made to Dr E. C. Godée-Molsbergen, *Reizen in Zuid-Afrika in de Hollandse Tijd* ('s-Gravenhage, Martinus Nijhoff 1916)

4 *Journal of Jan van Riebeeck* vol. I (Cape Town, van Riebeeck Society 1942), quoted in A. J. H. Goodwin, op cit, p. 48

5 G. M. Theal, *History of South Africa*, (reprinted Cape Town, C. Struik 1964), vol. III p. 255

6 Ibid, p. 266

7 G. M. Theal, *Abstract of the Debates and Resolutions of the Council of Policy at the Cape from 1651 - 1687*, (Cape Town, Saul Solomon 1881), p. 212

Fig. 1 Namaquas (Elliott Collection, Cape Archives)

Fig. 2 Simon van der Stel's camp in the region of the Koperbergen
(Morrison Collection, Cape Archives)

Fig. 3 Queen Rebecca
(Elliott Collection, Cape Archives)

Fig. 4 A Namaqua family (from the Gordon Collection, Cape Archives)

8 G. Waterhouse, *Simon van der Stel's Journal of his Expedition to Namaqualand, 1685/6,* (London, Longmans, Green 1932), p. 113

9 A. W. Rogers: 'An Old Report on the Copper Field of Namaqualand', *South African Journal of Science* 1917, p. 150

10 Ibid, p. 151

11 The Amsterdamsche el equalled 688 mm, the Haagsche el was 694 mm, the Delftsche 683 mm and the Brugsche 701 mm

12 A. W. Rogers, op cit, p. 151

13 *J. A. de Mist – Memorandum containing recommendations for the forms and administration of Government at the Cape of Good Hope,* (Cape Town, van Riebeeck Society 1920), p. 217

14 G. M. Theal, *Compendium of South African History and Geography,* (Lovedale, The Institution Press 1877), vol. II p. 63

15 See P. L. Scholtz, *Die Historiese Ontwikkeling van die Onder-Olifantsrivier 1660 - 1902,* Archives Yearbook for South African History 1966 (II), (Cape Town, Government Printer 1966), p. 21

16 So-called after Dr H. Richter, first inspector of the Rhenish Missionary Society

17 G.8 – '54, p. 16

18 Col Robert Gordon, traveller, hunter and Commander of the Cape in 1795, named the Orange River (formerly known as the Great or Gariep River) in July 1779. Lieut William Paterson, traveller and botanist

19 G.8 – '54, p. 16

20 Another sample tested by Sir John Herschel yielded 65%

21 Supplement to *The Cape of Good Hope Shipping List,* 14/7/1843

22 F. C. Cornell, *The Glamour of Prospecting: wanderings of a South African Prospector in search of copper, gold, emeralds and diamonds,* (London, T. Fisher Unwin 1920), pp. 92-93

23 J. Backhouse, *Narrative of a Visit to the Mauritius and South Africa,* (London, Hamilton, Adams & Co. 1844), pp. 581-582

24 Supplement to *The Cape of Good Hope Shipping List,* 14/7/1843

Chapter 1

As a result of the activities of The Cape of Good Hope West Coast Trading and Mining Company, and of certain Frenchmen whom it was thought were interested in commencing operations in the far west, interest in the copper deposits of Namaqualand was revived in 1845, and early in 1846 a prospectus was published in connection with the formation of The South African Mining Company. In this prospectus it was stated that:

> The existence of valuable mines in South Africa, capable of yielding abundantly to a company established on sound principles, and properly worked, is a simple fact well known for some time in the colony, and perhaps to some individuals in England who take an interest in Southern Africa. Still, up to the present time, no proper effort has been put forth to work them, and their easily procured wealth has been allowed to remain dormant.
>
> So far back as the year 1790, the attention of the Dutch Government was called to this fact; and in 1791[1] an expedition set out, and returned in 1792, being 10 months absent; and from the specimens of Ore obtained about sixty miles beyond the Orange River, on the Borradaile River, laid before them, a piece of Copper Ordnance was cast, as related by the late Mr de Wit, and confirmed by Mr Adriaan Louw, who was on the expedition. In 1836-7, Captain, now Sir James E. Alexander employed by the Royal Geographical Society, in his report mentions those Mines and states in his Travels, published in 1838, many interesting facts relative to them, consequent on which, in 1843, the outlines of a Prospectus to form a Company to work them, was published in the *Cape of Good Hope Shipping List, No. 183,* and some movement was, at the same time, made in London for the same purpose, founded on Sir J. E. Alexander's report, who as a preliminary, advised a careful survey of the Mine. There, however, the matter has been suffered to rest until now, when some Foreigners are endeavouring to get possession of, and work, one of the Mines of Copper near the Orange River. This has led to an examination of this Mine, and the result is:
>
> In 28 degrees, 40 minutes South latitude, and 17 degrees, 8 minutes East longitude, there is a mountain of Quartz, on the surface of which are earth and stones, impregnated with oxide of Copper, and on penetrating about two feet into the mountain, the interstices between the strata which lie nearly perpendicular are full of rich Ore, yielding, as proved by Sir John Herschel and others, from 28 to 65 per cent of pure Copper.[2]

Following the publication of this prospectus a letter was published from a certain J. B. Harrison '...trusting it...(might)...be the means of preventing the enterprizing public from a loss through the ignorance of adventurers, or from entering into a ridiculous speculation without due consideration'.[3] This letter was accompanied by a

'Report of the supposed Copper Mine, in the S.W. Coast of Africa, 1846', by a Capt. John Davies, a mining agent from Cornwall – addressed to J. B. Harrison, Esq., of Liverpool:

Dear Sir, – Having been called upon by you, to search out the *'Copper Mine District'*, so named by Capt. Alexander, and other travellers, and to report thereon, – and having proceeded on the coast, and into the interior as far as you deemed necessary, I beg *faithfully* to report thereon.

I have diligently and faithfully examined every part within the following boundaries, viz: from the mouth of the *Orange River* some twenty or twenty-five miles southward, and from thence some sixty miles eastward; comprizing a district of at least 1 200 square miles, – in which district iron ores abound in large quantities, both in regular 'lodes' and irregular 'masses'. The ores are worth from 25 to 40 per cent, but as no coals can be found here, it cannot be recommended as a mining speculation. I have not, however, seen the least indication of Copper Ore except at the place called on the Colonial Map, 'RICH COPPER MINE', situated south of the Cow Island, Orange River, from fifteen to twenty miles; and from the mouth of the said river, from fifty-five to sixty miles – the nature and appearance of which I shall briefly describe in the following manner –

The Copper Ore in question occurs on top of a small Hill, rising some eighty feet high; not in a vein or lode but as by mere accident, in a mass of hard quartz; and in so small a quantity, that if the said *hill* were smelted I do not think that 10 tons of copper could be obtained. I have certainly found here, small pieces of copper ore worth from 25 to 30 per cent, which I beg to hand you along with this report. However, very few pieces of this description can be had, since the quartz is merely oxidized with copper. And to geologically describe it – the 'BLUFF', or top of the *hill* is a layer of hard *quartz rock*, not at all congenial to copper, under which mass is a lyer (sic) of geniss (sic), having for its base hard granite.

As to this rich Copper Mine *district*, I beg to remark that for many miles around, it consists chiefly of irregular ranges of granite hills, with occasional layers of geniss, (sic), mica, mica-slate, quartz rock, etc., without a lode, vein or any strata; either indicative of gold, silver, mercury, zinc, lead, tin, copper, or any other metalliferous mineral. Nor can any man who understands the nature of mining be mistaken as to these matters, since both *hill* and *dale* are completely freed from sand, soil, and vegetation.

Deep ravines also occur in almost every direction, occasioned by the annual *torrents*, showing at once to the Miner, Mineralogist and Geologist, the nature of this district, without digging, boring, blasting, or removing any rubbish.[4]

In reply, Thomas Fannin,[5] the Honorary Secretary of The South African Mining Company, commented as follows:

...from the report of the 'Mine Agent from Cornwall', it appears that he has not even seen, much less 'faithfully examined', the mine near the Orange River, in which the mining company intend commencing operations. He may have seen *a* mine, but certainly not *the* mine. It appears the expedition brought out all the necessary tools and materials for a proper examination of the mines, but from the time they landed the wagon and tools at the mouth of the Orange River, misfortune attended their every movement,...the party got into the hands of the Frenchmen who have been endeavouring to get possession of the mines. They were their guides to the mining district pointed out by Sir James E. Alexander, showed them what answered their purpose, and never lost sight of the mining adventurers from Liverpool until we find both parties in Cape Town.[6]

Fannin commented on the reasons for the publication of this report:

I can only...pity the motives which induced...(Harrison)...to place such statements before the public, intended evidently to mislead them on a subject of such serious importance to the commercial interests of the Colony;...however...unfortunate in all the movements of the adventure by the *Ellen German*, the managers of that disastrous expedition would thus endeavour to hide their ignorance and misfortunes, by trying to prejudice the public mind against the operations of a company which would certainly...(expose)...the failure of the *Ellen German's* adventure.[7]

The publication of this letter appears to have taken its toll of potential investors since the original prospectus had mentioned an amount of £1 per share as being more than sufficient to '...prove what can be done, and enable the Directors to bring the ore into the English market, and show the Proprietors the value of this investment,'[8] while a revised prospectus issued on March 20, 1846, that is some 14 days after the publication of Harrison's letter, stated that the shareholders would run no risk beyond the deposit of 10s per share.[9] In addition, at the first meeting of the company a resolution was passed that the capital should consist of 2 000 shares of £10 each, whereas originally it had been proposed that the capital should consist of 5 000 shares of £20 each.

In another of the Cape papers, Dr Eveleigh, Professor of Physical Science at the South African College, gave his reasons for thinking that the conclusions at which Capt. Davies had arrived were false. He thought that the mine superintendent or mineralogist, who was not trained in the principles of geology, was unsuitable for the task of exploring unfamiliar terrain in search of mineral deposits.[10] However, Dr Eveleigh himself appears to have had but a slight knowledge of geology since he stated in the same letter that the barren state of Namaqualand was one of the most confirmatory proofs of the existence of metallic ore and coal – an extremely unsophisticated approach. Dr Eveleigh had not yet even visited Namaqualand at this time; he had, however, worked out a theory concerning its mineral deposits. He considered that this theory was corroborated by Capt. Davies' evidence.

According to Dr Eveleigh, the south-western part of Africa formed part of an immense basin. If South Africa lay on the opposite verge of the same basin as existed in South America, then there was every reason to suppose that the same minerals might be found in South Africa as in South America. And, if the Cornish miners were unable to appreciate the wealth of the South American mines because the ore was found in different circumstances from those prevailing at home, then they were equally ill-equipped to ascertain the merits of the South African mines.

The editor of *The Shipping and Mercantile Gazette* was meanwhile prompted to write an extremely bullish editorial, stating as 'fact' that copper ore of rich quality existed in at least six places in South Africa; that it was on the surface and that no attempt had yet been made to follow it down more than two feet; that native labour was readily and cheaply available to work the mine near the Orange River; that the carriage of the ore from the mine to the shipping port (Peacock Bay) was comparatively easy and cheap; and that the deposit near the Orange River was at the same degree of latitude and similarly circumstanced as ores found in South America and South Australia.[11]

Of the above 'facts', only one can be said to have been established without doubt – namely, that the ore had not been followed further than two feet, the depth to which Fannin had actually probed. The information in this editorial can only have been obtained from Fannin; it is substantially the same as that presented by him at the first meeting of The South African Mining Company held some seven days later. Thus, the editor of *The Shipping and Mercantile Gazette* can be seen as having given bullish reports on behalf of The South African Mining Company. Since he had been the Honorary Secretary of the proposed Orange River Mining Company of 1843, perhaps he also had some interest in The South African Mining Company.[12]

A few days later, the report of Dr C. C. Rykvoet to Ryk Tulbagh, 1762, was reprinted in the local press. Thomas Fannin promptly reacted, giving his reasons for believing that Dr Rykvoet's conclusions were no longer valid. To Rykvoet's objection that the rock was of an uncommon hard substance, and that its excavation would thus prove extremely laborious, Fannin replied that this was exactly the type of rock (quartz) in which copper was to be found, and was found in South America and South Australia where mines were being successfully worked. To the objection that there was insufficient wood in the vicinity to smelt the ore, Fannin replied that the ore was sufficiently valuable to carry the expense of carriage without smelting. Finally, to the objection that the Orange River would be unsuitable for transporting the ore by water because of many reefs and shoals, that in any event a harbour had still to be found, and that land carriage would be prohibitive, Fannin replied that the Orange River could be used for transportation and that the expense of carriage '...will not be half as much as compared with most mines'.[13]

The first point of interest which emerges from the above is that there would seem to be no reason to suppose that Rykvoet's mine and Fannin's were one and the same. However, this aside, Fannin's first comment seems of no relevance since whether or not the hardness of the rock was conducive to the presence of copper, the difficulties connected with working a mine in such rock would still remain. One cannot really say anything about his second comment except that this did not prove to be the case. But with regard to his third comment, his expectations were far too sanguine. He had at that stage not personally inspected the route to the coast and was thus not in a position to be so categorical about the matter. His statement as to the expense of carriage was completely false.

The first meeting of The South African Mining Company was held in the Commercial Hall, Cape Town, on March 21, 1846. A report of the company's proceedings to date was read by Fannin, who gave the following as the basis for formation of the company:

> From the concurring testimony of various travellers into the interior of South Africa, from 1762[14] up to this time, we have clear evidence of the existence of various ores on the surface of this continent.
>
> We have similar testimony that the like ores are found exactly similarly circumstanced on the continents of South America and South Australia, where the mines are successfully worked at the present moment.
>
> To Copper ore attention has been particularly directed, which from its intrinsic value,[15] as generally found in mines, will bear the heavy expenses of carriage to market, without smelting. Some pieces of this ore proved on analysis to contain from 28 to 65 per cent of pure copper, the average proving over 40 per cent.[16]

The company was actually carrying on where The West Coast Trading and Mining Company had left off, and was thus heavily reliant upon Alexander's report on the mine near the Orange River. Acting on Fannin's suggestion, it was decided to make a survey of the mine in order to determine the exact locality of the mine or mines, the geological position of the ore, whether anyone had attempted to discover the quantity of the ore, the availability of labour, the means which could be employed in getting the ore to the coast, the existence of a safe harbour and the ownership of the territory in which the mine was situated.[17]

Thomas Fannin, who was selected to conduct the survey, left Cape Town on December 1, 1845 in a light ox-wagon, and reached the Wesleyan Mission Station at Kamiesberg on December 20. There, with the assistance of the Rev. Mr Bailie, he enquired into the habits, customs, mode of living, and working of the Namaqua/Coloured population.

He arrived at Kommagas on December 24, where he received a friendly welcome from the Rev. Mr Schemelen, from whom 'most valuable' information was obtained:

> ...and on the object of the journey being fully entered into and explained to Mr Schemelen, he acknowledged the great benefits likely to result to the natives from the working of the mines on the proposed plan, viz., by a large body of shareholders, with a large capital, and carrying out every movement on straight-forward, upright principles, – paying the labourer just and fair wages, – and not, as in some former trading transactions, grasping all the produce of the country, for which mere trifles were given in exchange; and not only so, but unprincipled men spreading debauchery and infidelity wherever they went, thus counteracting the labours of the Missionaries.[18]

Mr Schemelen seemed confident that the Orange River mine would prove the most advantageous to work, but, as it was not too far out of the way, Fannin decided to see if it would be practical to bring the copper ore to the market from the copper mountains marked as such on Arrowsmith's map of the Colony, utilizing the bed of the River Kousie (which was at that time the official boundary of the Colony) as a road. To ascertain this he

> ...rode forward, on the 26th December, to the Kousie River, now dry; – but during the months of June, July and August, it has from two to seven feet of water flowing along its nearly level bed, from the mountains to the sea; its breadth varying from twenty to two hundred yards; the distance from the copper mountains to the sea being about sixty miles. Rode along the course of the River, the bed of which is in many places full of rocks, rendering it in its present state an impassable path; and as there is no safe harbour near here on the coast for shipping, no progress could be made in bringing the produce of those mines to the market at present.[19]

Fannin, together with his guides, one of whom was a certain Abraham Josef, a son of William Josef, named by Alexander,[20] reached the mine on the Orange River on December 31, 1845 – '...a hill of white flinty rock about one hundred yards high' – thus enabling Fannin to make his report on the questions noted above. We shall, however, confine ourselves to a consideration of only three of the most important questions.[21]

Firstly, with regard to the state of the labour market, Fannin commented as follows:

Native labour may be obtained through the influence of the missionaries, certain and abundant. The Orange River mine is centrally situate (sic) to the four mission stations of Kamiesberg, Kommagas, Kok Fontein, and Nisbet Bath, at each of which stations are hundreds of civilized Hottentots. Many of the young men have received a good education, know the value of wages, and beneficial employment, and are in every respect admirably circumstanced for assisting the company in working the mines...It may here be remarked that the Hottentots are accustomed to use the mattock in tilling their gardens; this tool is similar to a miner's pick, which they can be readily taught to use, and under proper management they will make good miners without requiring many workmen from England. Nor will it be necessary to erect dwellings for those workmen, as they invariably live in their own huts, formed of reeds and mats, which, with all their furniture for an entire family, may be carried on a single ox, and thus they wander from place to place. The farmers pay them wages from 3 to 10 rix-dollars per month,[22] and rations. Cape sheep may be purchased there for two or three shillings each, – oxen proportionably cheap, and there is abundance of water and corn land in the neighbourhood; so that there is no difficulty, but may be easily overcome, in procuring labour.[23]

This did not prove to be the case and the difficulty of securing labour proved to be a major obstacle. While Fannin blithely informs us that the Orange River Mine was centrally situated to the four mission stations, in fact the distance between them was fairly considerable. And, one wonders, since this area was beyond the borders of the Colony, just how accustomed the inhabitants really were to the payment of cash wages. Certainly a long time afterwards it was complained that they were not prepared to take up paid employment, preferring instead the freedom of living on their reserves.

Fannin stated that he had encountered no White farmers north of the River Kousie, a fact which is certainly not favourable to the suggestion that the indigenous inhabitants were accustomed to wage labour.[24] Perhaps, since Fannin had enquired into the working habits of the Namaqua/Coloured at the mission station of Kamiesberg, he obtained a false impression of their aptitudes and inclinations, as this station was within the borders of the Colony.

Secondly, with regard to the existence of a safe harbour on the coast, Fannin stated that there was one at Peacock Bay some six miles south of the Orange River, and that this had been proved by the landing of a wagon there by the brig *Ellen German*. He had not, however, at this stage personally inspected this bay, and so this was merely conjecture on his part.

Lastly, as to the rights of 'natives or other parties' to possession of the district where the ores were situated or through which they would have to be carried, enquiries were made of various 'authorities',[25] the result being that as far as could be established '...no tribe or individual *whatever* has any claim, worth a straw, to any part of the district between the Kousie and the Orange River'.[26] This seems utterly ridiculous since there were tribes in effective occupation who had been inhabiting the territory since time immemorial. Of course it was another matter as to whether the Government would recognize the claims of the indigenous inhabitants. Even if their rights to the land were recognized to a limited extent in the end, their rights to the mineral deposits were never recognized. So in this sense Fannin's conclusions were not far from the kernel of the matter.

Fannin arrived back in Cape Town on January 20, 1846. On the basis of his recommendations, it was decided to form a joint stock company to be known as The South African Mining Company. To this end the advice and co-operation of the Government was sought and Fannin records that he was examined before the Governor and Council on the subject, '...after which the Prospectus was published'.[27] The subsequent annexation of Namaqualand by Sir Harry Smith in December 1847, leads one to wonder whether this was not an early example of the flag following trade....

At the first meeting of the company Fannin not only presented a report on his activities to date in regard to exploratory work, but also gave details of the proposed mining operations, drawing attention to the following points: firstly, that no heavy adits would be required to convey water from the mouth of the mine; secondly, that unlike the situation in England where deep shafts had to be sunk before the lodes or veins were reached, here this would be unnecessary as the ore was close to the surface; thirdly, that because open-cast mining was possible, it would not be necessary for prospective miners to undergo extensive training, thus these miners could be found within the Colony, so avoiding both expense and delay in opening up of the mines; fourthly, that in the first instance no expense would be incurred in purchasing the mine, and so it was proposed that one tenth of the net profits were to be reserved for such a contingency; fifthly, that all tools and equipment required could be obtained in Cape Town; and finally, that the shareholders would run no risk beyond an initial deposit of 10s per share, and three months notice would have to be given prior to any further call. Solicitors were to be appointed to draw up a trust deed that would limit the liability of shareholders and leave it optional if they wished to retire from the concern before a second call was made. The directors were given notice that they were not to expend a greater amount than £1 000 without the consent of a general meeting of the shareholders. The following were elected as directors:

Baron von Ludwig (Chairman)
Edward Chiappini
Isaac Chase
William Billingsley
L. H. Twentyman
Edward Eager
George Thompson
Thomas Andsell
John King

Preparations were made to commence mining and a party was equipped for such an enterprise. On June 9, 1846, Fannin left once again for Namaqualand accompanied by an engineer, a miner, and the necessary staff.[28] The purpose of this second exploratory expedition was to confirm and augment the information derived from the first, since the first examination had been carried only two feet into the upper crust of the hill and could thus only be regarded as superficial. The best means of transport to the coast was also to be investigated.[29]

The party arrived at the mine on September 7 and mining was commenced within seven days. By the 22nd of the month the shaft was already eight feet deep and a vein some 14 inches wide had been struck.[30] Progress was rapid, but this was vital if a supply of funds was to be ensured. Fannin thought that the best way to open up the mine would be to drive a level or adit through the base of the hill, rather than quarrying from the top. With the limited means at his disposal (particularly inadequate labour), the latter course would have been impractical since it was likely that the whole of the available resources would have been exhausted before the ore body was reached. So, in conformity with his instructions and in order to satisfy the shareholders who doubted the existence of ore in quantity, it was deemed advisable to get some out as speedily as possible by following it down from where it appeared in greatest quantity on the surface.[31]

As the shaft was pushed downwards the ore was found in what are called 'bunches', growing larger and richer as they proceeded. Green carbonate was found nearest the surface and grey sulphide deeper down. Samples were then despatched to Cape Town by four different means, viz., by Thomas the smith[32] who said he was returning to Cape Town, by Mr Homewood, by the *Challenger* and by the *Speculator* which was lost on her way down. Only the sample conveyed by Mr Homewood reached the directors. That sample yielded 70%.

Fannin's next duty involved ascertaining the best means of conveyance to the coast. There was, it appears, a wagon path from the mine to the sea, but using it would have taken four days. Since he considered that ten tons could be transported on the Orange River as easily as one ton on the overland route, he concluded that transport via the Orange River was the only practical course. He personally inspected this route and commented

> ...although...(the tale)...can be told in a few words, I trust I will never again have to endure what I suffered in this survey from intense heat, thirst, and hunger.

How others were supposed to undertake this journey regularly to convey the ore to the coast one might wonder.

While at the mouth of the Orange River, during the first week of January 1847, Fannin received various letters

> ...from the Directors and other friends in Cape Town, advising me of the great anxiety of many of the Shareholders to see the ore in Cape Town, and desiring the transmission of five or ten tons or as much as possible without delay.[33]

This was considered necessary, because although his ' "Report and Survey of the 'Copper Bergen' and the River",[34] did spread new and good hopes into the veins of some of the Shareholders,'[35] Baron von Ludwig, the Chairman of the Company, considered that it was essential to forward a few tons of good ore at the earliest opportunity in order to convince the shareholders that work was being done on their behalf. In a letter to Fannin, von Ludwig stated that, as soon as Fannin had remitted a few tons of copper ore, he intended calling together a general meeting of the shareholders to propose a further small advance on their shares as the capital of the Company was almost exhausted.[36]

Because of the difficulty in procuring labour, Fannin found it impossible to mine five or ten tons of ore as requested and ship it to Cape Town. He was therefore reduced to attempting this overland. He tried unsuccessfully to obtain the assistance of some of Paul Lynx's[37] men and others who were in the neighbourhood, but he was forced to ride to Kookfontein (Steinkopf) and on to Kamiesberg before he was able to obtain the services of three men to bring the ore to Kamiesberg, and the promise of others to drive it on to Cape Town. This last proved necessary since at Kamiesberg he had received instructions to return to Cape Town by the fastest possible means – horseback – and leave the ore to follow.

His presence was required in Cape Town for the second meeting of the Company. In concluding his address to this meeting, Fannin commented

...I will conclude by expressing a hope that no further delay will occur in working the mine we now possess, satisfied as I am that the exports of precious metals from this Colony will soon be larger than all its other exports added together.[38]

The prices of the shares of The South African Mining Company are rather illuminating as a gauge of the interest shown in the activities of the Company.

Share Price List of The South African Mining Company[39]

Date	*No. of shares*	*Nominal value*	*Amount paid up*	*Market value*	*Dividends*
21 Mar 1846	2 000	£10	10s	18s	none
26 Feb 1847	2 000	£10	10s	10s	none
May 1847	2 000	£10	£1	£1	none
10 Mar 1848	2 000	£10	£1	£0	none

In May 1847, at an adjoined public meeting of the Company, a further 10s per share was unanimously voted in order to enable the directors to continue operations, and in the *The Mercantile and Shipping Gazette* of May 28, 1847, a notice was published of a meeting to be held on the following day to decide upon the adoption or rejection of the agreements to commence working about to be entered into with a party of miners.[40]

Nothing further appears to have been done in connection with this. A new announcement of the value of Shares in Joint Stock Companies in *The Shipping and Mercantile Gazette* of April 28, 1848, does not include The South African Mining Company. It should be noted that the shares had already ceased to have a quoted market value in March of that year. The third annual general meeting of the company should have been held around this time. This meeting does not appear to have taken place and this may account for the shares becoming valueless. The company appears simply to have faded out of existence for a few years without ever having been formally dissolved.[41]

NOTES TO CHAPTER 1

1 This is a reference to the expedition led by Willem van Reenen which left Cape Town on September 17, 1791 and returned on June 20, 1792
2 *The Shipping and Mercantile Gazette*, 27/2/1846
3 *The Shipping and Mercantile Gazette*, 6/3/1846
4 Ibid. This report was the result of exploratory work conducted during an expedition known as the 'adventure of the *Ellen German*'. A brig, the *Ellen German* had landed a wagon and all the implements necessary for mineralogical exploration at Peacock's Bay early in 1846. The report was the result of Capt. Davies' explorations
5 Not much is known of Thomas Fannin. However, there are some details of personal history in an article by M. G. Fannin entitled 'The First Attempts at Mining in Namaqualand', in *The Mining and Industrial Magazine*, 7/3/1928
6 *The Shipping and Mercantile Gazette*, 6/3/1846
7 Ibid
8 *The Shipping and Mercantile Gazette*, 27/2/1846
9 *The Shipping and Mercantile Gazette*, 20/3/1846
10 G.8 – '54, pp. 23-24
11 *The Shipping and Mercantile Gazette*, 13/3/1846
12 Silberbauer poured eulogies upon the Company which seems to have had something in common with the philanthropic missionary aims of The West Coast Trading and Mining Company
13 *The Shipping and Mercantile Gazette*, 20/3/1846
14 It is interesting to note here that in the original prospectus issued in February no mention was made of this testimony of 1762, the company, being stimulated to exploratory work solely by the opinion of Alexander, and the van Reenen expedition of 1792, although in fact van Reenen obtained the ore he brought back with him from north of the Orange River. (G. M. Theal, *History of South Africa*, vol. IV p. 258). Perhaps, even if the promoters of The South African Mining Company had known of the existence of Rykvoet's report they would not themselves have drawn attention to it because of its pessimistic nature. In the event it is clear that the originators of the Company based their interest in Namaqualand solely upon the evidence of Alexander, and were thus led astray in disregarding the deposits of the Springbokfontein area, which it was considered were unexploitable because of the difficulties in regard to transport
15 Perhaps this 'intrinsic' value referred to was thought privately to represent more than copper. We refer to evidence brought forward by Dr Eveleigh to prove that he was the first person to discover the existence of gold in Namaqualand. He stated in a sworn affidavit given on February 16, 1854:
'I, George Eveleigh, do hereby solemnly and sincerely declare that, in the month of March, 1846, a Mr R. C. Jones gave me a specimen of "Copper Ore", which he declared had been brought from the North part of the division of Clanwilliam which, on chemical examination, I found to contain a small quantity of Gold, which I produced in the presence of Mr Jones and others. That, on producing this in the presence of the Directors of the South African Mining Company, they requested me to repeat the experiment on a larger scale in their presence, or of their Secretary, which I did, and obtained nearly two grains of Gold from one

hundred grains of the Ore. And I further declare that I gave a globule of the said Gold to the said Secretary, for the satisfaction and information of the Directors of the said Company, and another globule I retained in my own possession.' See G.8 – '54, pp. 22-23

16 *The Shipping and Mercantile Gazette*, 3/4/1846

17 Ibid

18 Ibid

19 Ibid. The Kousie empties itself into the sea approximately midway between the harbours of Hondeklip Bay and Port Nolloth. Thus Fannin was correct in asserting that there was no suitable harbour close to the mouth of the river. His mistake lay in choosing the most direct route to the sea

20 J. E. Alexander, op cit, vol. I p. 117. William Joseph was referred to by Alexander as his 'copper-indicator', ibid, vol. I p. 253

21 The other questions have been dealt with in passing. See pp. 19 and 22

22 At a value of 1s 6d per rix-dollar, this would have been from 4s 6d to 15s per month

23 *The Shipping and Mercantile Gazette*, 3/4/1846

24 Though we know that there were Whites living beyond the border of the Colony, and perhaps even beyond the Orange River itself, by the beginning of the nineteenth century, the number of Whites doing so was so small one cannot conclude that wage labour was a custom of the indigenous population

25 Rev. Dr Phillip, the Rev. Messrs Hodgson, Jackson and Shaw, of the Civil Commissioner at Clanwilliam, Mr Ryneveld, of the Dutch Boers encountered south of the River Kousie, and most important of all, the Rev. Mr Schemelen

26 Though only a short time later a certain McDougall considered it necessary to obtain a lease from a Khoi chief to work deposits which must have been extremely close to those of The South African Mining Company

27 *The Shipping and Mercantile Gazette*, 3/4/1846

28 *The Shipping and Mercantile Gazette*, 12/6/1846

29 *The Shipping and Mercantile Gazette*, 30/4/1847

30 *The Shipping and Mercantile Gazette*, 6/11/1846

31 *The Shipping and Mercantile Gazette*, 30/4/1847

32 'At the mines some work was done and rich Copper Ore opened up, but the two Welsh miners soon grew discontented with the lonely life, and, in the end, when a vessel from the Cape touched at the mouth of the Orange River, they returned by her.' M. G. Fannin, op cit, p. 17

33 *The Shipping and Mercantile Gazette*, 30/4/1847

34 This report was published under the title 'Orange River Copper Mine', in *The Shipping and Mercantile Gazette*, 6/11/1846

35 M. G. Fannin, op cit, p. 18

36 Ibid, pp. 18-19

37 Paul Lynx was a Namaqua chieftain who claimed suzerainty over large tracts of Namaqualand

38 *The Shipping and Mercantile Gazette*, 30/4/1847. It is noteworthy, however, that Mr Fannin sold his interest in the Company soon afterwards and bought a farm in Natal with the proceeds. Thus his faith in the prospects of the Company could not have been very great

39 Compiled from various issues of *The Shipping and Mercantile Gazette*

40 *The Shipping and Mercantile Gazette*, 28/5/1847

41 That the Company was not formally dissolved is shown by the fact that when it recommenced operations in 1854, notice was given that those who had not paid the second instalment voted in May 1847, would be allowed to continue their shares if they paid this within three months of notice being given in the Gazette (*The Shipping and Mercantile Gazette*, 17/2/1854)

Fig. 5 A Namaqua group as depicted by Charles Bell, illustrating 'civilizing' influences (Elliott Collection, Cape Archives)

Fig. 6 A well-to-do farmer in Namaqualand 1925 (Cape Archives Acc715)

Fig. 7 The *Bosphorus* (Elliott Collection, Cape Archives)

Fig. 8 Springbokfontein 1854 (from a sketchbook in the Library of Parliament, Cape Town)

Chapter 2

Some time after the disastrous expedition of The South African Mining Company a German named von Schlicht went to Namaqualand and discovered by chance that on the farm Springbokfontein, alias Melkboschuil, alias Koperberg, there existed an immense deposit of copper ore which '...stuck out of the mountainside in full view like a huge vein'.[1]

Von Schlicht returned to Cape Town '...to proclaim the good news',[2] but he was unable to interest either the investors or the merchants of Cape Town in this venture. In light of the failure of The South African Mining Company this was hardly surprising. John Blades Currey ascribed the lack of interest in von Schlicht's discoveries to the popularity of Sir Walter Scott's novels, for in Scott's novel *The Antiquary*, von Dousterswivel, a charlatan who induced Sir Arthur Wardour to invest large sums in fictitious copper mines which almost brought about the downfall of the Wardour family, was a German.[3]

At this time von Schlicht lived with a man named Jencken whom he naturally told of his discoveries. When von Schlicht was subsequently absent from Cape Town for a number of years, Jencken, who was in business with the support of the firm of Phillips & King, got into difficulties. In order to repay his principals, he offered to go to Namaqualand to open a general store and at the same time to investigate von Schlicht's discovery – an offer which was accepted by Phillips & King.[4]

Jencken sent such glowing reports of these deposits at Springbokfontein that Phillips & King decided to send up a Mr John Wild, in whom they had complete confidence, to investigate further. He supported Jencken's observations entirely, and so the business of '...Copper mining or rather Copper gathering was entered upon'.[5] No publicity was sought for their activities, however, since they were not sure what action the Government would take in the matter. Sir Harry Smith had extended the boundary of the Colony up to the Orange River in December 1847.[6] Therefore Springbokfontein fell within the sphere of the Cape Government. At this time, title to the farm had not yet been granted to the occupiers, the Cloete brothers, to whom it was granted only on January 21, 1850.[7] No mineral rights were retained by the Government. We may be sure that this would not have been the case had the Government known of the existence of valuable deposits of copper ore.[8]

Von Schlicht had meanwhile returned to Cape Town. Learning that Jencken was in Namaqualand, he realised that it was his discoveries which had taken that gentleman there. Getting together with two of his friends, von Schlicht promptly set off for Namaqualand or, more precisely, the farm Springbokfontein. On arrival there, they apparently found large stacks of copper ore awaiting shipment. Taking advantage of the temporary absence of John Wild, they immediately entered into negotiations for the purchase of the farm. These negotiations were apparently well advanced before they all retired for the night, promising to conclude their business in the morning, but

...while they slept Mr Wild who always travelled by night came home and he was not a man to let the grass grow under his feet. A glance at the neat Cape Town travelling wagon told him enough, and getting in at the back door of the house he quietly roused the farmer and his wife and at sunrise he met the travellers with a smiling face and the deed of sale of the farm in his pocket.[9]

How literally John Blades Currey's description of events should be taken is debatable. What is known is that on March 16, 1850, the purchase price of £50 was paid, while the deed of sale for the portion purchased – which was ten morgen, 351 sq. roods – was formally completed on October 28, 1850 at Melkboschuil, and that this document was in fact witnessed by H. D. Jencken and John Wild.[10]

By this document Phillips & King obtained the mineral rights to the entire farm and, in addition, sufficient land for the erection of any buildings and works that might be considered necessary for the working of any future mineral discoveries. They were also granted the right to graze any cattle, horses, goats and sheep they might require for the working of the mine or mines; the right to the use of water; and the rights of free access and making roads. The remainder of the farm was subsequently acquired by Phillips & King for the sum of £2 344 10s.

Von Schlicht, in conjunction with J. W. Stoll a hatter of Cape Town, and representatives of the firms of Thomson, Watson & Co., and Prince, Collison & Co.,[11] engaged in further prospecting work. Finding that other rich deposits existed, but upon Crown land, they entered into correspondence with the Government, requesting permission '...to search and work for the same'.[12] The Government had only shortly before stated in a reply to J. H. van Reenen that it was not in the power of the Government to '...make any such grant or lease of land for the purpose of mining or otherwise, as you propose. The Crown lands of the Colony can be alienated only by sale, at or after a public auction,'[13] but it was now decided that it lay within the Government's power after all to grant leases, based upon the Australian model, for the purpose of ascertaining and developing such mineral resources as existed on Government lands in Namaqualand.[14]

Notwithstanding the economic crisis which had existed in Cape Town only a short time before, as a result of over-trading and speculation with the gold regions of Australia, and which had seriously threatened to involve some of the most respected of the Cape mercantile houses and apparently did make the 'money market' inconveniently tight for some time,[15] the Cape, and especially Cape Town, indulged in a mania of speculation following the publication of a proclamation of September 13, 1853, relative to the issue of leases for mining of non-auriferous metals in Namaqualand.

To some extent the copper mining mania was probably the direct consequence of the news that had filtered through to the Cape of the Californian and Australian gold discoveries. Having searched in vain for gold here the public, on learning that the Cape Town firm of Phillips & King were making a 'handsome thing' of copper in Namaqualand, decided to 'go nap' on copper. The mania might also have resulted in part from a prevailing lack of investment opportunities.[16]

It was generally believed that the copper lay close to the surface in vast quantities of high grade, a belief expressed in the description of these potential mines given by Blancheton, the French Consul at the Cape, in his *Vade-mecum* describing the Cape exhibits at the Paris Exhibition of 1855:

> When we reflect that the numerous copper mines recently discovered in Namaqualand extend, almost without interruption, over a surface of from 8 000 to 9 000 square miles, at all degrees of depth, and that the ore is found almost everywhere at the surface, so that it may be collected the greater part of the time above ground, we may come to the conclusion that this country is destined to produce annually more *copper* than all the mines in the world united.[17]

Credence was given to the assertions that Namaqualand was one great mineral bed by the rather rose-coloured report on the mines by A. G. Bain, a belief which tempted some to seek centres for mining in the office of the Surveyor-General rather than on site.

Bain refuted the accusations levelled at him which suggested that his report had caused persons to sink their funds in following an *ignis fatuis* all over Namaqualand. He claimed that in his one and only report on the subject, printed in 1854 as part of the *Papers and Correspondence on Namaqualand*,[18] he had spoken flatteringly only of the Spectakel, Springbok and Concordia mines and, furthermore, that events had not disproved such flattery.[19] The general tone of his report was, however, extremely optimistic:

Let the farms be cultivated and the mines opened, and it will be found that Namaqualand contains more real wealth than the whole Colony put together; for I have little doubt that all the country from the Oliphant's River to the Orange River abounds in mineral wealth, and only wants to be thoroughly explored to develop its riches.[20]

That his report gave people confidence in the prospects of Namaqualand is illustrated by the following resolution passed in June 1854 by a meeting of gentlemen interested in the mineral lands of Namaqualand:

That in the opinion of this meeting, any doubt of the correctness of the various statements as to the existence of rich deposits of copper ore in Namaqualand is entirely removed by the concurrent testimony of many gentlemen, well known for their strict integrity, among whom may be named Mr Bain.[21]

The testimony of Charles Bell would also seem to bear out the conclusion that the generally optimistic nature of Bain's report was responsible for creating great excitement amongst the investors of Cape Town:

...(I arrived in Namaqualand)...with highly excited ideas of inexhaustible wealth, for, in this office here, I had heard much of it; and I had read Mr Bain's Memorandum, as to what he saw on the southern border. Had my observation been limited to the same range, and had my fellow citizens of Cape Town been less excitable, this report might have been couched in the same strain, for I saw nothing to damp my high expectations at Springbok and Concordia, nor, perhaps, at Spectakel, on my return, in another condition of body, and, consequently, in another frame of mind.[22]

Thus it can be seen that even the Surveyor-General was put in a highly excited frame of mind by Bain's report.

The alleged value of copper ore was, however, not the only stimulating factor. Aware of the discovery of gold in Australia and California, the public became imbued with a '...craving lust, for sudden and extraordinary wealth',[23] caused by rumours that gold had been discovered in the Sovereignty,[24] and great excitement prevailed when a certain Mr Nicholls who had been in the employ of Phillips & King, claimed the reward of the Gold Discovery Committee[25] for having discovered gold in Namaqualand.[26]

These rumours caused an increase in the value of shares on the market at that time, i.e. early in 1854, most notably those of The

South African Mining Company and The Cape of Good Hope Mining Company,[27] although the excitement was described as a hoax by *The Cape Monitor's* mining correspondent. Apparently people in Namaqualand knew so little of the gold fever raging in Cape Town that the news took them by surprise, and Nicholls was given the cold shoulder since he could not lead those who went with him to any definite spot where Namaqualand gold could be found.[28] As a result the shares were soon at a discount.[29]

A factor which gave stimulus to the boom was the generally held belief that investors in England would, on being assured of the abundance of copper ore in Namaqualand, purchase the mining centres at any price.[30]

This naturally enough gave rise to the searching out for, and leasing of, as many centres as possible; and some companies possessed large numbers – one had 60 or 70 and was still searching for more.[31] The low rentals encouraged this form of speculation.[32]

Attempts to interest English investors failed. Having burnt their fingers only shortly before in the Australian mining boom, they were rather more cautious this time. In an article in *The English Mining Journal*, reprinted in *The Cape Monitor*, investors were warned strongly against investment in the Namaqualand companies. Describing the history of the Australian companies, it was noted that the promoters of these Australian gold companies had promised immediate dividends to the fortunate allottees who were to become rich overnight. The result had been that not one company had paid a dividend, most had either wound up their affairs or become defunct in discreditable circumstances, while those still in existence were carrying on a protracted struggle for survival. It was considered that investment in Namaqualand was equally speculative, sharing the same dangers and drawbacks, the greatest weakness in the development of both areas being the employment of incompetent agents: '. . . many of whom knew nothing of mining or labour previous to their arrival at the scene of operations.'[33] This is well illustrated by evidence given by Mr Chiappini before the Select Committee on Mineral Leases, 1856, when he pointed out that with regard to the Great Namaqualand Mining Company, a gentleman sent up as manager of the mines soon wrote to the directors at Cape Town informing them that he had come across a 'splendid' lot of about 80 tons. On examining a sample of this ore, the directors also thought it to be very good. When examined by an authority, it was found to contain not a particle of copper.[34]

The implication of *The English Mining Journal* was then, that the Namaqualand companies suffered from the same defects as the Australian ones which had recently failed, and that the Namaqualand companies would suffer the same fate as their Australian counterparts. In this it was correct.

In describing the means likely to be used by these Namaqualand mining companies to obtain capital from England, a satirical commentary was given:

The companies will be probably got up in the usual stereotyped manner – the directors an Irish peer, some decayed baronet, several honourables, a ruined merchant, a crafty solicitor, &c., all of whom will, no doubt, for their names, receive a certain percentage, and several thousand free shares, which they can dispose of at premiums in the market. A secretary who can pay a portion of the preliminary expenses will obtain the situation, and some relative of the governing body, without the least knowledge of mining, will be sent out to the colony, to take the direction of affairs. In nearly every instance this has been the case with our foreign mining adventures, and the consequence has been that, although the directors and *employés* have benefited, the shareholders have found their money expended, not in the legitimate prosecution of the undertaking, but in the enrichment of a few individuals, who, on the faith of their names and supposed high character, have extracted large amounts of money from the public, which they have themselves engrossed.

We will not further allude to the conduct of many of these public bodies, whose infamy is now so notorious. We wish to see enterprise fostered in South Africa, but we emphatically caution the public from embarking in schemes where the only security they obtain is high-sounding names, and where incompetent agents are likely to be employed. Those men may possibly rig the market, and run up the shares for a few days; but it will be done at the expense of the company. They have nothing to lose, but all to gain. Such associations should be avoided. Money should be invested in those associations where the directors are men of business and standing, and thereby able to guarantee to the public that they will look as ably and conscientiously after their affairs as they do with regard to their own.[35]

With the example of the Australian mining mania cautioning them and being warned by knowledgeable persons at home, it is not surprising that English entrepreneurs were not anxious to invest in Namaqualand. Current monetary conditions also did not favour foreign investment; for, with the imminence of the Crimean War, the bank rate had increased to approximately 5-5½% by 1854, thus making speculative ventures aboard unattractive. Despite the fact that it had decreased to 3½% by June 1855, the failure of many of the companies to date made investment highly speculative. In any case, by October the bank rate was once again 5½% and remained high for some time thereafter.[36]

The Cape public were continually warned of the dangers of indiscriminate speculation, even though any person who '...suggested a question that was calculated to bring an unsatisfactory answer was scouted as an enemy to the colony'.[37] Many of these warnings were contained in the extremely flowery language of the time:

At the beginning of the week, the violence of the South-Easter kept everybody within doors who was not absolutely compelled to traverse the streets; and thus induced a short abatement of the Mining Share Fever. This epidemic has, however, recovered its power, and reigns and rages literally 'like a house on fire', a conflagration which must now spend itself, and end only by burning itself out.

Unhappily, those best qualified to suggest and apply (or, if need be, enforce) a remedy, are themselves among those who have been attacked most violently. And the tedious convalescence of those who escape present destruction, will, it is to be feared, prove as fatal as the disease itself. A disorder of such virulence, and attended with such long and unintermitting delirium, such perplexing alterations of nausea and ravening hunger, must reduce the constitution to an ebb, from which the greatest care and skill will hardly effect recovery. Among some patients the understanding exhibits symptoms which lead to the apprehension of permanent mental aberration. Others have been effected in a different way, and seem to have lost the functions of sound business health, and the taste and the capacity for ordinary pursuits; and, in not a few cases, a moral obliquity of vision has appeared, (as there are some men who do not possess the power to perceive certain colours) which disables the sufferer from recognizing or appreciating some very distinct shades in the ethical spectrum.[38]

Perhaps, however, the warnings were so veiled by rhetoric that they were not taken seriously: whatever the cause, they were largely ignored.

There does not seem to have been any control over the setting up of companies, and so, especially at the height of the boom late in 1854 when the majority of the companies were formed, many raised capital upon the most meagre and vague information. The Henkris Mining Company, for example, was formed upon the following:

HENKRIS MINING COMPANY

PROSPECTUS

The proprietors of certain Nine Centres, to be leased from the Colonial Government, and which have been applied for on the selection of Mr J. A. Bam, Jr., who has personally visited Namaqualand, and brought to town with him samples of Surface Ore, gathered from these Centres, propose to form a Company, to be called the 'HENKRIS MINING COMPANY'.[39]

On the basis of the above 'prospectus' the originators of the company proposed to receive applications for shares to the amount of £15 000. This capital was then to be split in such a way that the originators, who did not exceed half a dozen, would possess £8 500 and the subscribers £6 500 of the capital. Thus the subscribers would be paying a premium of more than 100% for entering a company which had done nothing besides exhibiting a few ounces of *surface ore* – samples which had not even been examined by a competent mineralogist – from centres selected by a gentleman whose credentials, if any, were not given. 'Asmus', *The Commercial Advertizer's* correspondent commented:

> The most attractive part of the prospectus is probably the queer sounding title of the '*Henkris*' company, which may possibly be either *Sanscrit* or *Hottentot:* or as some believe, a Cockneyism for 'Increase'.[40]

Not content with the investment opportunities presented by enterprising Cape Town gentlemen, the public sought out promising private companies in the hope of persuading them to be allowed to participate, as may be seen from the preamble of the Prospectus of The Rietberg Mining Company, published in November 1854:

> In consequence of the numerous Applications for Shares, the Lessees of the Copper Mine 'Wheal de Villiers' (claim no. 248) have resolved to allow the public to participate in the working of the said Mine.[41]

This prospectus contains amongst others, the following points; a capital of £1 000 000 in 20 000 shares (and no more!) of £50 each to be offered; 5 000 shares were to be reserved for the lessees for their own benefit in remuneration for giving up *one-fourth* of the mine; the first four instalments on the remaining issue totalling £5 per share, making altogether £75 000 for the remaining three-fourths of the mine. If this was perhaps thought to favour the originators rather heavily, the public was at least given the benefit of knowing that its money would be put to good use, for the prospectus stated further that: 'Whatever profits the present lessees may derive will be principally appropriated to Religious and Philanthropic purposes.'[42] The offer was, however, withdrawn by a notice published the following week, the lessees having in the meantime been convinced that '...it would be too heavy a charge on the financial means of this colony to work such a Copper Mine well'.[43]

The deplorable gullibility of the public led one caustic citizen (probably the editor) to insert the following 'prospectus' in the pages of *The Cape Monitor:*

ADVERTISEMENT

LADIES' MINING COMPANY

PROSPECTUS

Several young ladies, who have made a tour to Namaqualand (in imagination), are desirous to make known their discoveries to the Wives and Daughters of their fellow-citizens of all classes.

The scheme on which they purpose to commence their work, will be, not only as avowedly honest and safe as many of those started before, but the Projectors assure their Sister-citizens, that they know as much of the NAMAQUALAND METAL (Brass) as many of those who have previously projected Mining Schemes. There will be no need of either Tramway or Railway for bringing their Metal from the Country, and its value is so well known to Speculators, that the Projectors feel no analysis of Samples is necessary. It is proposed to issue THREE MILLION SHARES, at A SHILLING each. Sixpence to be paid previous to any information being given of the Whereabouts of the Mines, and the other sixpence when the Mines produces anything beyond the first Sample. The Directors will be appointed previous to the First Meeting taking place (as is usual); and no old Women or Apprentices will be allowed to have any Share in the undertaking. If all the Shares should be taken up before Applications can be sent in from the Country, the Original Proprietors will not hesitate to issue a few Extra on their own responsibility.

Some excellent hands at 'Stagging' are engaged, and nothing will be left undone that legitimate trading in Mines will admit of. The First Meeting will take place on ROBBEN ISLAND. Queen REBECCA is engaged to propose the First Resolution.[44]

Offices: Kable Court
Treasurer: Agnes Stretchem
Solicitors: Mesdames Fleece'em & Do'em
Secretary: Sarah Scrip

While in another newspaper the following advertisement appeared:

LUNAR MINING COMPANY

Notwithstanding all the Shares in the Lunar Mining Company having been taken, and the first, second, and third Instalments readily and willingly paid, the late proprietors, still feeling intense interest in the Scheme, have much pleasure in informing the Shareholders that they are in treaty with a celebrated Optician for the purchase of an Instrument of much greater power than the best Refractor, through the agency of which the Moon can be brought down to the Earth, and the working party, now formed, be enabled to scrape the Copper off the surface.

The advantages thus offered to the public over other Companies cannot be too highly appreciated, when they are informed that all this is surface Copper, so perfectly pure, that no smelting is required, and it displays, in addition, undoubted proofs of the presence of Gold. The plan of a tramway being thus happily superseded, the fourth or last Instalment will not be required. It is therefore proposed by the Directors to give the Shareholders the immediate benefit of the immense saving thus effected; and as no more notices will be issued, they are requested to call for their dividends at 326 St. George's Street, now due, but not payable.[45]

The investment criterion of the public is difficult to understand. Indeed the psychology of investors during boom periods defies analysis. *The Cape Monitor* commented upon this in August 1855, i.e. after the bubble had burst.

Companies, who started without knowing where they were to work, or without knowing if ever they should be enabled to get centres, have since then secured centres of some sort, and found 'indications' of metallic deposits. This at least has been the case, we believe, with all the companies, started without anything beyond a prospectus and a secretary's name at the bottom of it. When the companies had nothing the public had faith. If the public here have a 'mind's eye', it was strangely dazzled by glittering delusions, just at the time when premiums were given on nothing. The brass of prospectors glittered like gold, when 'lit up by the sun of promise', as poets would say. They who said a word about 'dupes' were stigmatized as 'no friends to the colony'. Into journals that brought out no 'puffs', no advertizements were sent by many of the companies. It was an extraordinary time. Nobody would be undeceived. They cherished the deceits practised, in the most unaccountable manner, and fondled deceivers most encouragingly. Now the tables are turned; but if the deceived were asked why? They could not answer. Companies that had done nothing, have since sent agents to explore, who return and report favourably; but they who listened, when the companies promised without exploring, will not believe now. All the credulity, called faith, is gone. It was founded on nothing and it has evaporated. There has been something most extraordinary in the conduct of the public on this matter. It was worse than chasing a bubble. There was no bubble. They chased without.[46]

But, while a company such as The Henkris Mining Company was able to attract investors sufficient for its establishment, The Namaqua Mining Company with its headquarters at Concordia was not. In their prospectus which appeared in September 1854, it was proposed that 10 000 shares were to be created, the proprietors retaining 5 000 shares, and the remaining 5 000 shares of £20 each were to be issued to the public.

Of seven calls which it proposed to make, the first, amounting to £25 000, was to be used to improve the works at the mines, the second, third and fourth, amounting to £37 500, were to be used exclusively to improve the means of transport, either by taking shares in the proposed Tramway Company, or by doing whatever seemed most beneficial to the interests of the company. The last three calls, also amounting to £37 500, were to be paid to the proprietors as compensation for giving up a half of their mining interests, which also included the working capital – this had apparently involved some £7 000 – and the cutter *Ceres*, as well as all the ore sorted and unsorted lying at the mines. But, since it was proposed that these last three calls be made from the profits of the company, the shareholders would have had to bear only four calls directly.[47] What is more, in a detailed report on the probable profitability of the mines put before the public in November 1854, some seven weeks after the appearance of the prospectus, it was suggested that the final three calls would not be appropriated by the proprietors, but instead be added to the funds to be raised for the formation of a Railway or Tramway Company in London.[48]

Operations had been in progress some time before it was decided to form a public company. And, shortly before the publication of The Namaqua Mining Company's prospectus, an advertisement had appeared in the press calling for tenders to be submitted for the transport of 1 000 tons of ore to the coast for shipment.[49] Thus in this case the public were offered the opportunity of investing in a company which was already established, and furthermore one which had been highly praised by A. G. Bain in his report:

I next visited the mines of Prince, Collison, Watson, & Co., at a place near 'Tweefontein', now called Concordia. These are also exceedingly rich, but, unlike the other mines I had visited, had something of the appearance of immense lodes running in an Easterly and Westerly direction, yet from their length, breadth, and depth, seemed inexhaustible. Here I saw some of the richest and most beautiful specimens of copper pyrites, peacock, and malachite, &c., that I had any where met with. For miles around this favoured spot, strong indications of copper every where appear; and a large village is in the course of construction, in which hundreds of happy families may yet reside. Much activity prevails here, as well as at Phillips and King's mines, but more in the way of building than of mining, as transport to the coast is not at present to be obtained, even at very high prices.[50]

However, the public proved unwilling to take up the shares offered in this company. Therefore notice was given in January 1855, that since the required number of shares (4 000) had not been subscribed for, the proprietors were withdrawing their offer to the public.[51]

The reason for lack of public interest in this company is probably to be found in a letter from the correspondent for *The Grahamstown Journal* which attacked this company most strongly:

The central group of mines may be called those of Concordia, belonging to Prince, Collison & Co., and those in that neighbourhood, from whom appeared some time since an advertisement for transport for 1 000 tons of ore! This, believe me, was all a flame, and a hundredth part would have been nearer the mark. The mine is, however, a very fair one, and will no doubt under careful management pay its expenses. A clue, however, to the advertisement has since been found in a circular, proposing to form a Company with a capital of £200 000, the whole of which was to go eventually into the pockets of the fortunate holders of the mine. Blind, however, as the public generally are, this time they had their eyes open, and the scheme appears to have fallen to the ground. Concordia is not, nevertheless, as we said before, at all a bad mine, and if it had only a better supply of water, good roads, and a little pasturage in the neighbourhood, its central situation would be much in its favour. The nearest shipping place to this mine is Robbe Bay.[52]

Despite the editor of *The Cape Monitor* rejecting these allegations and giving prominence to the fact that ore from these mines had been assayed by Sir H. T. de la Beche, '...the world renowned mineralogist', and found by him to be extremely rich – containing a large percentage of copper of the first quality – and further that a Mr Jidd, who had some connection with *The English Mining Journal*, had certified that '...*better foreign ore has not reached England*',[53] at last the public appears to have taken to heart at least one of the warnings concerning indiscriminate speculation.

It must be pointed out in fairness that the company by its own calculations had only about 100 tons of ore awaiting shipment[54] and, furthermore, that from the figures presented in a statement of probable profitability it seemed more than likely that, without some improvement in the means of transport, the annual profit would amount to only about £1 000, a very low return on the investment. If reliance had to be placed on ox-wagon transport, it was considered by the proprietors that '...the copper mines would...become of little or no value'. Since the majority of the subscribers to other issues were persons who were not planning upon, and indeed in most cases would have been unable, to pay up the nominal value of the shares for which they subscribed, then it is plain to see why a company, which was decried by the comment that it would '...no doubt under careful management pay its expenses' failed to find favour with a public mad about 'glamour shares'.

The companies were usually formed either without possessing any mining centres[55] – in which case they might be further divided into those which intended securing such, and those which did not – or else they were formed by taking over the assets of a private group, the so-called proprietors or originators who, as the promoters of such an undertaking, would obtain a certain percentage of the share capital.

In either case, the methods by which centres were selected left much to be desired. In most cases they were selected by people of 'integrity' but with no knowledge of geology, and in Namaqualand, where surface indications abound, great care was necessary in the selection of any sites. Unfortunately, the generally held belief was

...that no operations were needed to raise ore, nor would there be any operations required for a (great) number of years. It...(being said)...that of surface ore there was sufficient to employ all the labour of the colony for a great number of years.[56]

This belief, within the context of the general unsuitability of the persons who were entrusted with the selection of these centres, led to an over-emphasis on surface indications, with disastrous results. As Andrew Wyley in his *Geological Report of 1857* had pointed out, many of the hard granite or gneiss bosses showed a brilliant stain of green on their joints. This derived from the fact that being so much more impermeable than the softer and decomposed rock around them, into which copper impregnation could easily flow, a thin crust was deposited upon the surface of the harder rocks. The realisation of this fact by early prospectors for copper in Namaqualand would have prevented many mistakes for, in fact, it meant that the more brilliant the stain, the less chance of finding copper in the rock.[57] That 'Heath Robinson' methods were used to seek copper indications is evident when we encounter such tales as the following:

...we have...(for example)...the origin of the Dog's Ear Company, who are unsuspectingly outlaying on red paint...*Hondeklip* literally translated means Dog-stone, and Hondeklip derived its name from a large stone likened to a dog, which is there found. A traveller some years ago, having no better amusement, painted the stone red. The weather has however cleaned the surface of it, and the paint is all off except in the crevices, where it just appears. A Prospector, sent down by one of the companies, mistook these red spots for indications, and so knocked off the dog's ear and sent it home to his employers, who cherish it as the foundation of their hopes, and shew it as a prize, which the shareholders inexperienced in mineralogical science, rely upon in perfect faith.[58]

It was common practice to employ Namaquas to search out and secure centres, even the redoubtable Dr Atherstone being forced into utilizing this indigenous prospecting service:

Our...(difficulties in regard to exploration)...were also very much increased by the positions of centres already applied for being so vaguely defined as to render it almost impossible to recognize the locality intended, and also by the fact that previous explorers frequently put up no beacons at all, or placed them purposely in positions where they could not be seen, generally at a distance from, and often out of sight of, the 'indication' on which the centre was taken; so that after a hard day's work we had the mortification of finding that we had been re-discovering indications on centres already applied for! Finding that much valuable time was likely to be consumed in this unprofitable kind of research, I hired a native well acquainted with all the centres previously applied for, (and through whose instrumentality I believe most if not all of them had been obtained) to guide me to some spot which no person had yet visited, promising him also that if he succeeded in finding an indication which should be considered worth working, that the sum of £7 10s should be paid to him. As he did succeed in discovering an indication, I consider myself pledged on behalf of the committee to pay him this sum in the event of this centre being leased. I afterwards made a similar arrangement with another native, who is now I believe hunting for centres upon the same terms, which he promised to retain for us until Mr Damant's return. This I found was the plan commonly adopted by the agents of the different companies in that part of Namaqualand, – most of the indications being discovered by natives in the first instance: in fact the task of clambering up these rugged ridges in the summer months must be to a European almost a physical impossibility.[59]

Scientific methods were not thought necessary for the discovery of ore bodies. It was considered that if Phillips & King could come across rich mines by chance without scientific assistance, so could anybody else, luck being completely discounted as a contributory factor.[60]

The boom period spans a number of years – from the proclamation of September 13, 1853, until early in 1855. Certain peaks occurred during this period, the first in the early months of 1854, when in March, for example, the shares of The Cape of Good Hope Mining Company reached £4 each – at this stage 10s per share had been paid up – and the Company had not as yet obtained any centres (however poor those they later obtained might have been). Shares in The South African Mining Company reached £10 2s 6d – at this stage £1 per share was paid up (being the £1 advanced in 1847). The South African Mining Company had decided to revive its operations in February 1854, a board of directors having been elected only shortly before.

All the excitement was based on a rumour spread by a certain Mr Nicholls, concerning the discovery of gold in Namaqualand.[61] When no gold could be found, the shares soon fell in value. Rumours regarding the existence of gold interspersed with Namaqualand copper persisted, however,[62] leading to concern on the part of the Lieut-Governor who feared that these rumours would lead to a sudden and unwarranted influx of population.[63] A second and more sustained peak occurred late in 1854, when the majority of the companies were formed – none of which, it might be added, survived the mining mania. From the time of publication of A. G. Bain's report,[64] i.e. from about July 1854 to January 1855, some 22 companies were formed.[65] Paradoxically, even while share prices were falling every day, people were still prepared to invest in companies whose '. . . shaft sinking was never intended to be deeper than the breeches' pocket of their victims'.[66] During this period, enormous premiums were paid for shares in companies which had done little besides obtaining a number of centres and, often, not even this.[67]

Late in 1855, when it appeared certain that most, if not all, the companies would fail, a suggestion made by Blancheton in his *Vade-mecum* was given some attention. He had proposed that while late in 1854 there existed some 30 or 40 companies, each in competition with the other, taking into consideration the difficulties in regard to transport, the scarcity of labour – especially of experienced miners and overseers – it might have been more sensible to have placed all the mining operations under a '...*general company of copper mines in South Africa*, with a central administration, composed of elective members, acting in mutuality'.[68] Anticipating the crash, he suggested that, without waiting for the force of events to assist in the fusion of the companies, a general company should be formed, '...founded on the principle of *unity of action in the centralisation of ways and means*,...(which)... might produce practical results, in perfect harmony with the special conditions of separate existence and progress to each of the companies, considered independently'.[69] He was thus proposing a sort of early version of the mining-group system.

Plans were then put forward to form an Amalgamated Mining Company as being the only way to salvage the capital sunk in the various concerns, and a prospectus in regard to such a company appeared early in 1856.[70] These plans did not materialise. Almost all the companies went into liquidation until by 1857 only three of them survived – the two private companies; Phillips & King, and The Namaqua Mining Company, and one public company; The South African Mining Company[71] although the latter also disappeared within a short space of time. A. G. Bain, who was so largely responsible for the mania, subsequently commented rather light-heartedly:

> There have been a series of mineral and metallic monomanias of late at the Cape. The first was the coal, the second the copper, and the third the golden mania. Of the copper mania it has been truly observed, that it had shewn a wonderful aptitude for the diminution of tin in this colony, the latter metal doubtless having amalgamated with the former to form a sort of spurious brass, an article so much in demand by some of the numerous mining companies.[72]

It was at one time estimated that a sum of about £100 000 had been locked up in the share market.[73] This figure was subsequently estimated not to exceed £70 000,[74] most of this being subscribed by men of very limited means. The shareholders, because of their belief in the illimitable wealth of the Namaqualand mines, had not anticipated paying up the full value of their shares. Many had expected to receive dividends upon their deposits,[75] and, as a result, among the shareholders were to be found '...apprentices and errand boys not out of their teens',[76] leading one commentator to observe that, if one-third of the nominal capital of all the companies was to be called up, the shareholders would not be able to meet the calls. It was not that there was insufficient capital within the Colony, but rather that the majority of the shareholders would be found to be defaulters.[77]

Apart from the sum lost through being tied up in the share market in subscribing to the issues, an even greater amount was lost

> ...that which has been realized to some pockets out of others in the shape of premiums. There is scarcely any calculating the extent of that sum. Shares changed hands, some of them ten times a day, and each time with a profit. These profits, although they are not now locked up, have chiefly passed out of business into the hands of another class of men altogether.[78]

In a subsequent assessment of the situation, it was determined that everything had not been quite so straightforward:

> There has not...(however)...been the amount of money sunk, that persons who only hear the tales about eighteen hundred pounds, and two thousand pounds, premiums, would be led to suppose. The chief part of the enormous premiums were paid in bills, that have never been taken up; putting down the gold for scrip has been rare. Some, it is true, gave very high premiums, in hard cash, but these cases were exceptions. The rule was, where high premiums were given, to give bills with the hope of turning the transaction over a few times before the bill became due, and so contriving to scheme the necessary amount for the bill, with a profit for the dealer. Those who gave bills, were persons without means. If the bill became due before they had sufficiently realized on the scrip, it was either renewed or dishonoured.[79]

So great was the dabbling in scrip that the suggestion was made it should become legal tender.[80] Although the copper mining mania occasioned a great deal of activity, the stagnation in trade which followed the collapse of the copper bubble can hardly be described as a full-scale economic depression. It must be attributed not only to injudicious dealings in shares but also to the falling off of demand from country districts as a result of horse and cattle sickness prevalent at the time.[81]

This boom must be viewed as an inevitable concomitant of a particular period of development amongst all nations and parallels in South African history the South Sea Bubble in England, as a factor contributing to the growth of a modern, capitalistic, credit economy.[82]

NOTES ON CHAPTER 2

1 J. B. Currey, *Half a Century in South Africa,* (Ms, South African Library), p. 95
2 Ibid, p. 95
3 Ibid, p. 96
4 John King, of the firm Phillips & King, had been one of the directors of The South African Mining Company, and must therefore have known about the existence of these deposits, since they were mentioned by Thomas Fannin in his reports, which may well have been a factor favouring their acceptance of von Schlicht's offer
5 J. B. Currey, op cit, p. 96
6 Proclamation of 17/12/1847
7 It was one of 11 farms granted, the deed being signed by Sir H. G. Smith. The quitrent amounted to £4 per year on the 21 410 morgen. The farm was granted in equal portions to the seven brothers: Nicolaas, Jan, Gert, Jacobus, Piet, Dirk and Jacob Cloete
8 See *The South African Commercial Advertizer and Cape Town Mail,* 26/8/1854
9 J. B. Currey, op cit, p. 97
10 Agreement dated 28/10/1850 filed in the Deeds Office, Cape Town, together with Deed of Transfer No. 197, dated 26/12/1850. The sale was in the following proportions:
3/6ths to Silvanus Phillips, John King and Charles Phillips
2/6ths to Peter Clarke Daniels, and 1/6th to James King
Peter Clarke Daniels subsequently transferred his shares:
½ of 1/6th share to Phillips & King on 23/5/1852
½ of 1/6th share to Phillips & King on 25/5/1852
11 In October 1853 they formed themselves into The Namaqua Mining Company
12 G.8 – '54, p. 1
13 C.O. 4393 No. 151, Col-Sec. to J. H. van Reenen, 10/9/1852
14 G.8 – '54, pp. 1-2
15 *The Cape Monitor,* 16/9/1854
16 J. E. Alexander, op cit, vol. II p. 280
17 E. Blancheton, *Vade-mecum,* (Cape Town, Saul Solomon 1855), p. 57
18 G.8 – '54, pp. 35-37. This report was also published in various newspapers, among them, *The South African Commercial Advertizer and Cape Town Mail,* 16/11/1854
19 *The Cape Monitor,* 5/1/1856
20 G.8 – '54, p. 37
21 *The Cape Mercantile Advertizer,* 24/6/1854
22 G.8 – '55, pp. 18-19
23 *The Cape Monitor,* 16/9/1854
24 G.8 – '54, pp. 20-26. Considerable excitement prevailed in Cape Town especially during 1854, as a result of the alleged discovery of gold in South Africa. Rumours were put about concerning the discovery of gold in Namaqualand, but these were soon discounted. A far greater attraction was the Smithfield diggings. So much excitement was created by the alleged discovery of gold in the Sovereignty (Orange River Colony) that *The Cape Monitor* even had a column devoted to 'Chronicles of the Cape Diggings', in which some space was devoted to Namaqualand, but the major portion of which was devoted to the Smithfield diggings

25 See Eric Rosenthal, *Other Men's Millions*, (Cape Town, H. B. Timmins 1953), pp. 21-23 for a description of the founding of the Committee for the Discovery of Gold

26 G.8 – '54, pp. 20-21

27 See p. 46

28 *The Cape Monitor*, 11/3/1854

29 *The Shipping and Mercantile Gazette*, 14/4/1854

30 Rev. W. Holden, *History of the Colony of Natal*, (London, Heylin 1855), p. 441. *The South African Commercial Advertizer and Cape Town Mail*, 2/12/1854

31 Rev. W. Holden, ibid, p. 441

32 G.8 – '55, p. 26

33 *The Cape Monitor*, 21/4/1855

34 S.C.5 – '56, p. 13

35 *The Cape Monitor*, 21/4/1855

36 R. G. Hawtrey, *A Century of Bank Rate*, (London, Longmans, Green 1938), p. 281

37 *The Cape Monitor*, 26/12/1855

38 *The Shipping and Mercantile Gazette*, 10/11/1854

39 *The Cape Mercantile Advertizer*, 29/11/1854

40 *The South African Commercial Advertizer and Cape Town Mail*, 2/12/1854

41 *The Cape Mercantile Advertizer*, 6/11/1854
See also the prospectus of the Koper Kop Mining Company, *The Cape Mercantile Advertizer*, 30/10/1854

42 *The Cape Mercantile Advertizer*, 6/11/1854

43 *The Cape Mercantile Advertizer*, 13/11/1854

44 *The Cape Monitor*, 4/11/1854

45 *The Cape Mercantile Advertizer*, 13/11/1854

46 *The Cape Monitor*, 8/8/1855. The Rev. W. Holden in his *History of the Colony of Natal*, p. 441, gives the following extract from a newspaper account:
'The proprietor of the lease of three or four centres disposes of them on the following conditions:– five thousand shares are to be created of £5 each, of which he is to receive one thousand shares without paying a sixpence, and out of the first profits (!) the sum of £15 000. Would you credit that the company was formed in less than an hour, that the following day 5s *per* share was paid, and that in the course of a fortnight they were selling at £5 per share?'

47 *The Shipping and Mercantile Gazette*, 29/9/1854

48 *The South African Commercial Advertizer and Cape Town Mail*, 16/11/1854

49 *The Shipping and Mercantile Gazette*, 21/7/1854

50 G.8 – '54, p. 36. Quoted in the Prospectus of the Company, see *The Shipping and Mercantile Gazette*, 29/9/1854

51 *The Cape Monitor*, 6/1/1855

52 *The Cape Monitor*, 30/9/1854

53 *The Cape Monitor*, 14/10/1854

54 *The South African Commercial Advertizer and Cape Town Mail*, 16/11/1854. There was about 1 000 tons lying at the mines, but most of it was of too low a grade to bear the existing rates for transport

55 *The Cape Monitor*, 24/2/1855

56 *The Cape Monitor*, 3/2/1855

57 G.36 – '57, p. 29

58 *The Cape Monitor*, 30/12/1854

59 Dr G. Atherstone: 'Namaqualand and its Mining Prospects', *The Eastern Province Monthly Magazine*, vol. II no. 13, Sept. 1857, p. 5. It is perhaps interesting to note that this report upon Namaqualand had already been submitted to the Grahamstown Prospecting Company in February 1855; perhaps the delay in its publication had something to do with its pessimistic character. In reply to a rhetorical question, viz. 'Can the ore be worked and shipped *at remunerative prices?*' he answers: '*In the present state of the country*, without rail or tramway, and with no foreign or sufficient colonial capital to assist in developing the resources of the country, I am of opinion that it *will not pay;* and I fear that any single unaided company that attempted it would only be expending capital to benefit later adventurers by their experience. I would strongly recommend that no expenses whatever be incurred *at present* beyond what is necessary for having the centres already applied for fixed and surveyed' (pp. 7-8)

60 *The Cape Monitor*, 5/1/1856

61 See pp. 36 – 37

62 The existence of this gold interspersed with the copper of Namaqualand had been known for some time. For an interesting comment upon the question see the article by M. Delesse: 'Notice sur Les Mines de Cuivre du Cap de Bonne-Espérance,' in *Annales des Mines*, 5e serie, 1855, tome VIII

63 G.8 – '54, p. 8

64 Bain's report is dated 19/6/1854

65 More than 40 companies were formed altogether. See the Table of Companies (p. 133) and fold-out tables

66 *The Cape Monitor*, 23/12/1854

67 Some idea of the heights to which shares rose and fell might be gained from the table below:

Early December 1854	*Market Value*
Port Elizabeth Mining Company	£1. 0. 0. per share
Union Mining Company	1. 10. 0. per share
Victoria or Een Dop Mining Company	1. 0. 0. per share
Equitable Mining Company	10. 0. per share
Cape Colonial Mining Company	11. 0. per share

August 1855 *Company*	*No. of Shares*	
Port Elizabeth Co.	75	These 510 shares were purchased for the sum of £7, they purported to represent £2 000 par (£190 paid up), and would have fetched in December 1854, £240.10.0.
Union Mining Co.	25	
Victoria or Een Dop Co.	40	
Equitable Mining Co.	310	
Cape Colonial Co.	60	

68 E. Blancheton, op cit, p. 60

69 Ibid, p. 60

70 *The Cape Monitor*, 5/1/1856. This contains a ten-point plan for an Amalgamated Mining Company

71 *The Cape of Good Hope Almanac and Annual Register for 1857*, (Cape Town, van de Sandt de Villiers & Co. 1856), p. 171

72 A. G. Bain: 'Geology of South Africa', *The Eastern Province Monthly Magazine*, vol. I no. 8, 1857, pp. 403-404

73 *The Cape Monitor*, 30/12/1854

74 *The Cape Monitor*, 27/10/1855. Subsequently it was suggested that as much as £200 000 had been sunk in mining speculation; see S.C.5 – '56, p. 40

75 *The Cape Monitor*, 19/5/1855

76 *The Cape Monitor*, 11/11/1854

77 Rev. W. Holden, op cit, p. 440

78 *The Cape Monitor*, 30/12/1854

79 *The Cape Monitor*, 29/8/1855

80 *The Cape Monitor*, 30/12/1854

81 *The Cape Monitor*, 28/5/1856

82 C. G. W. Schumann, *Structural Changes and Business Cycles in South Africa, 1806-1936*, (London, P.S. King 1938), pp. 77-79

Chapter 3

Sir Harry Smith, by a proclamation of December 17, 1847, extended the boundary of the Colony to the banks of the Orange River, thus including Namaqualand in the Colony. The inhabitants of Namaqualand had until then consisted almost entirely of Khoi, San and persons of mixed extraction, though Whites had already begun infiltration as early as 1750 when the first frontier farmers pushed into the desert wilderness that is Namaqualand.[1] Both Khoi and White were continually in a state of war with the San.

Prior to the entry of Whites upon the scene great insecurity of tenure had existed. There had been no fixed boundaries definitely separating one group from another:

> Individuals and families gathered themselves into tribes and clans, and resided in or frequented a particular locality, around which they were compelled, in self-defence, to create a desert proportionate to their power, so that they might not be taken unawares and at disadvantage. Individual property in land was unknown, and it would be no easy matter to define the ever expanding or contracting limits of the usual haunts of the tribe. Of course every now and then the time came when, by treachery, or skill, or strength, the desert was passed from without, a general slaughter ensued, and any survivors who might escape, took up a new position or otherwise became (in border phrase) broken men.[2]

The Namaqua were accustomed to roaming freely throughout Namaqualand, except where the San were congregated, and thus regarded almost the entire area of Namaqualand as their sphere of influence.

The nomadic life of the Namaqua and the unfavourable climatic conditions to which they were exposed resulted in the population being very sparsely scattered. This gave the first Whites to enter the territory the impression that the land was unpopulated. Thus they applied for loan farms from the Council of Policy. The first such grants were used only for occasional grazing, but, when boers later settled permanently in Namaqualand the Khoi felt deeply wronged.[3]

James Alexander commenting on the granting of farms beyond the Olifants River,[4] said that the information of the Cape authorities was very limited with regards to the geography of the Colony and that grants were awarded in so careless a manner that their titles were questionable in the extreme. In fact, many of these farms were not only beyond the Olifants River but beyond the boundary, a fact of which the applicants were, in his opinion, well aware when they applied. These farmers, he contended, continued to pay taxes so that they could lay a claim to colonial protection.[5] It should be pointed out, however, that the grant to Coenraad Feyt of the farm Cammasfontein, dated March 4, 1776, stated explicitly that the grant was on the banks of the 'Groote Rivier'.[6]

In any event, the instability in regard to tenure, and the lack of fixed borders, created a problem in regard to the rights of the natives of Namaqualand – a problem which came to the fore with the advent of mining in the 1850s. As early as 1842, a memorial was addressed to the Government by several inhabitants of the Missionary Institution of Steinkopf, remonstrating against a possible extension of the colonial boundary. In reply to this, it was argued that the Government had no intention of extending the boundary of the Colony '...or of interfering with the rights of those inhabiting the country beyond the boundary, by granting those lands to the colonial farmers',[7] although, as has been pointed out, farms had actually been granted many years previously to farmers as far away as the banks of the Orange River, and perhaps even beyond.[8]

When in 1846 the Government again made moves to extend the boundary, the native inhabitants were consulted first. The Chief of Steinkopf upon being asked, in the presence of the Rev. Mr Brecher, by the Fieldcornet Jacobus Kotzé, about his opinion of such a step, replied that: '...What the great chief or governor does, I cannot object to; but this only I say, that I will keep my ground, for me and my people, in order to lead a quiet and honest life.'[9] Although the territory was annexed in 1847 there was no officer of the Government stationed there, the missionaries and chiefs continuing to manage the affairs of the territory as before.[10] This must, of necessity, have meant that the missionaries and chiefs were unsure of their rights, but presumably they thought that their lands were secured since they had beneficially occupied them before the annexation of the territory.

In 1851[11] the Rev. Brecher addressed a further memorial to the Government on the question of the rights of the indigenous inhabitants to the possession of the mission lands:

The chiefs and natives residing here wish to be placed under the protection of the British Government, and that the ground occupied by them (a diagram of which is herewith forwarded) may be reserved for their occupancy, against the encroachments of farmers, traders, or any others wishing to settle on the same, as much unpleasantness has already arisen on this point. The chief or captain wishes, further, to ascertain how far his power extends over his own people, and also how he should act in such case of intrusion as above alluded to.

Your memorialist would further add, that the ministers of the Evangelical Church have laboured about 36 years amongst this people, and have been favoured by the Great Head of the church with much success; and that the people are worthy of the countenance, support, and protection of the British Government.

The number of natives at present residing here is about – (sic), possessing cattle, sheep, and goats; so that Your Excellency will perceive that the ground requested to be reserved is absolutely necessary for their support.

And, in conclusion, would humbly pray Your Excellency to take the matter into your consideration, together with the memorial relative to the station at Pella, and grant a favourable answer.[12]

In reply to the above memorial, and also in connection with verbal communication with the Rev. Brecher, John Montagu, the Colonial Secretary, stated that no ticket of occupation could be granted to the occupiers of Steinkopf. However, the Government would not

...countenance any encroachments on the land occupied by the people of the institutions...on the part of any farmers or others not belonging to the same; nor has His Excellency any desire to disturb them in their occupancy.[13]

Meanwhile, the 'Concordia Consortium',[14] finding that Phillips & King had acquired the deposits at Springbokfontein, conducted further exploratory work. Finding rich deposits of ore at Tweefontein, later called Concordia, they made representation to the Government in April 1853, in order to ascertain whether they would be allowed to search for certain minerals which they believed to exist in Namaqualand. They inquired from the Government, whether, if they should be disposed to work such deposits, the Government would be prepared to grant leases for this purpose and, if so, upon what conditions.[15]

In reply, the Acting Secretary to Government, William Hope, stated that having laid their request before the Lieut-Governor, he was empowered to say the Government would no doubt be prepared to grant such leases, most probably upon the same conditions as had been established in the Australian colonies, and immediate measures would be taken to ascertain what these were.[16] Secretary of State, Newcastle, approved of these interim measures and forwarded a copy of the regulations governing the Australian leases. Regulations to govern the Cape leases, modelled largely upon the Australian ones, were soon drawn up, appearing on September 13, 1853.[17]

Leases were to be granted for not less than ten and not more than 40 morgen to the first applicant, at a rate of £1 per morgen per year. These leases were to run for a total of 15 years, provided that a diagram of the ground was lodged with the Government within 12 months from the date of issue of the licence. During this 12-month period the potential lessee had the right of search upon land for a distance of one mile around the central point named in his licence, and the lessee could then select the most favourable spot. Provision was also made for the pasturing of cattle belonging to the lessees and they were to have the right of grazing for a distance of one mile radius for a lease of ten morgen, one and a half miles for 20 morgen, one and three-quarter miles for 30 morgen, or two miles for 40 morgen. This was to relate, however, only to '...ungranted or unleased Government lands'.[18] At the termination of the lease period, the land would be put up for public auction to the highest bidder; should the land not be purchased by the lessee, the purchaser would have to recompense the lessee for the value (to be estimated) of any improvements. The leases were to become void and forfeited for two reasons: firstly, if the rent was not paid in advance, and secondly, if the land was not applied *bona fide* to mining purposes. The conditions relating to this last safeguard were so vague as to be completely ineffectual, however.

Acting upon this information a company was formed by von Schlicht, Stoll, Thomson, Watson & Co., and Prince, Collison & Co. – The Namaqua Mining Company. Having obtained a lease to work the deposits discovered at Tweefontein, representatives were despatched there. On arrival at this place, they were greeted by a note of protest from the Rev. Brecher:

To Messrs A. von Schlicht, and
G. Prince, Tweefontein

Gentlemen, – Whereas I am informed by yourself of your settlement in the neighbourhood of the place called Tweefontein, for working copper mines, &c.; and whereas it was in your belief that the said place was situated without the institution-ground of Steinkopf; – on, however, making inquiry I find the same is situated, not without, but within the ground belonging to the institution.

And I beg to state that this mentioned ground is secured from Government against any encroachments on the part of any farmers, or others.

Therefore, gentlemen, I must, in the name of my community, and especially of the Captain Jacobus Engelbrecht, make objection against your settlement on our territory, and declare you, by this, to remove from the said place.

Should you, however, be unwilling to remove, then I trust you will be kind enough to inform the Government of the truth of the case. I must do the same, and we have reason to believe the question between you and us settled according to law. You will please give me a reply. – I remain, &c.

F. Brecher, V.D.M.[19]

As a result of this communication, and in order to safeguard their interests, The Namaqua Mining Company entered into an agreement with the Office Bearers and Members of the Institution of Steinkopf, whereby they were granted exclusive mineral rights to the Steinkopf Mission lands for a period of ten years.[20]

For this right, The Namaqua Mining Company agreed to pay the sum of £100 per annum; the lease to be renewable at the end of ten years. Payment was to commence only when exploitation began. The Namaqua Mining Company entered, so they claimed, into this lease because they thought that

> ...Mr Darling[21] had as much right to grant mineral leases to search for ore within ten miles of Paris or Berlin, as to search in native Namaqualand, without making the natives some compensation or coming to some understanding with them on the subject which gave him the right.[22]

It is possible that they were partly motivated by economic considerations, i.e. that a lease obtained from members of the Steinkopf Mission would be more favourable to their interests than one obtained from the Government. In any case, The Namaqua Company addressed the Government and desired to be informed of the facts of the case since it seemed to them that the members of Steinkopf Mission were within their rights to eject them from mission ground. The Company wished to know whether, if it should in fact be found that these people had not given up possession of their mission grounds, the Government would be prepared to refund them the rent paid to them, as otherwise a duplication of rent would have taken place.[23]

In reply, Richard Southey stated that whether or not The Namaqua Mining Company had entered into a lease with the people of Steinkopf was their own affair. Ownership of the land, he contended, was admitted to be in the Crown by the very documents which purported to show that ownership was in their hands of the members of Steinkopf Mission:

> ...(since)...otherwise the missionaries and native captain would not have applied to the Government for a ticket of occupation, and the only promise on the part of the Government was, that the natives would be protected from encroachments of that very nature which the terms of the lease include.[24]

In effect what this meant was that while the Government recognized the right of the indigenous population to the veld, they did not acknowledge their right to what lay beneath it. Since Namaqua/Coloured had not engaged in large scale copper mining before the annexation of the territory, their rights in respect to minerals were not recognized – this is explicitly stated in a letter to Rev. Brecher forwarding a list of persons who held mining concessions in Namaqualand:

> ...the grounds upon which the Government has based its right to dispose of the mineral resources of that country consist in the principle that, as mining was not one of the purposes to which the land was appropriated by the natives prior to the extension of the colonial boundary to the Orange River, so no ticket of occupation issued after that time could recognize any right in that respect on the part of natives, much less their power to alienate any such privilege, by lease, sale, or otherwise.[25]

The indigenous population were nevertheless to be compensated for the use of land and in respect of water and pasturage.

The Namaqua Mining Company, however, felt dissatisfied with the situation and so addressed the Lieut-Governor, Sir George Cathcart, by means of a petition which purported to come from the Captain, Commandant, Elders, members of the Evangelical Church of Steinkopf, and other inhabitants of Little Namaqualand. In this memorial it was stated that:

> We, your memorialists, beg humbly to bring to your Excellency's notice, that the land now belonging to the missionary institution at Steinkopf, has been the undisputed property of our forefathers and ourselves from time immemorial; that fixed places of residences were in existence nearly half a century ago; and when, in January, 1851, a memorial was sent to His Excellency Sir Harry Smith, at our request, by our respected minister, the Rev. Mr Brecher, we merely requested that we might be *taken under the protection of the British Government,* without having the least idea of relinquishing our just claim to the lands in this locality.[26]

It was thus requested that the issue of any mining or other leases within the limits of possession of the mission station be suspended until the merits of the case had been decided.

In reply to this petition it was stated that while the question of the rights of the indigenous population had not yet been settled, any private arrangements entered into in respect of lease or compensation could have no legal validity until some decision had been made as to the rights of these inhabitants; and even then their validity would apply only within the bounds of the rights or grants made. The Namaqua Mining Company, to ensure themselves of adequate pasturage, thereupon entered into an agreement with the Office Bearers of Steinkopf *re* the pasturing of cattle.[27]

While certain tracts were reserved for the indigenous population,[28] they were deprived of the mineral rights which were rightfully theirs. This was only finally settled with the passing of the *Mission Stations and Communal Reserves Act, No. 29* of 1909 which '...prohibited the "natives" of the territory from any legal claim to mineral rights on the land which was reserved for them'.[29]

At the height of the copper mining mania, tremendous numbers of leases were applied for, and it was confidently expected that the income from these leases would be some £3 000 per annum[30] – this being the rental on some 193 leases[31] (apparently application was made for some 2 000 centres[32]). However, within a short time most of these leases were forfeited through non-payment and, since Government Notice of September 13, 1853, was withdrawn by Government Notice of February 2, 1855, no new leases could be issued.[33]

In 1856 a Select Committee was appointed to consider a petition from leaseholders of land in Namaqualand who desired an extension in the period of the leases from 15 to 33 years, a renewal of the right of search, and an alteration in the means of payment from one of rents to one of royalty or export duty. The Committee came to the conclusion that the '...prayer of the Petitioners is reasonable and deserving of the consideration of His Excellency the Governor'.[34] This report is interesting as it marked very definitely the close of a period of speculative hysteria. Almost all the existing companies were represented and, it clearly emerges from the evidence, that most of these companies had undertaken very little real work. Evidence was given by the secretaries or representatives of 14 mining companies (excluding that given by the representatives of The Namaqua Mining Company and Phillips & King). These companies together had, it appears, exported by that time only about 41 tons of ore, of which two companies had exported 33 tons.[35] The secretaries or representatives of these companies, almost without exception, knew virtually nothing of the activities of their respective concerns. Most of them did not even know the date of formation of their companies, how many leases had been obtained – not to mention applied for, or what the expenditure had been upon those leases actually obtained.

Almost certainly, the desire of the companies for an extension of the lease period was founded upon the hope of being able thereby to dispose of these leases at a profit, rather than upon the often cited reason of inducing English capitalists to invest in a railway or tramway company.[36] Their desire for an alteration in the means of payment was also founded upon this hope, for the payment of a royalty or export duty instead of a rental would mean that the burden of holding large numbers of leases upon which no work was intended to be done would thereby be reduced. Their complaints of excessive rentals had no foundation since evidence given before the Select Committee clearly shows that, as a percentage of total expenditure, expenditure on leases was minimal.[37] In any case, the Government, in order to assist the companies, had prior to this agreed to the payment of what was described as a 'deposit' of 5s per morgen, instead of the stipulated rental of £1 per morgen. The Select Committee, in recommending the prayer of the petitioners, was almost certainly influenced by the hope that such accession would lead to a revival in trade. Unhappily the Government failed to act upon the recommendations of this Select Committee, leaving the question of right of search for mineral centres in abeyance for some years.

In 1864 another Select Committee was appointed to consider and report upon the system of leasing by the Government of the copper mines in Namaqualand, and the expediency of altering the same by levying a royalty upon the export of ore as an alternative to the rentals charged until that time. This Select Committee reported that leases should be granted for a period of not less than 33 years; that the area of the leases should be not less than ten and not more than 40 morgen; that for such leases the lessees should pay the Government a rental of £1 per morgen for the first year, this to be increased yearly by an amount of £1 until the tenth year, when, for the remainder of the lease the rent should remain fixed at £10 per morgen per annum; that every lessee should commence mining within one year of obtaining the lease; and that the conditions otherwise appertaining to the leases of September 13, 1853 be retained. As far as the existing leases were concerned, the Committee suggested that they should be extended for a period of 18 years upon the same scale of increasing rental. The Committee's only witness was the manager of The Cape Copper Mining Company whose recommendations they largely accepted.

The Government did not, however, adopt any of the Select Committee's suggestions. While Committee members had reported that the difficulties in levying a royalty and the expense of its collection rendered it inadvisable to adopt this mode of raising revenue from the Mineral Lands,[38] this was exactly the mode decided upon by the Government. Act No. 12 of 1865, which was an Act *Fixing the Terms upon which Mineral Lands in Namaqualand, the property of the Crown may be leased and worked*, provided for an annual rental of 5s per morgen, the extent of a lease not to exceed 40 morgen. In addition the lessee would also be required to pay the sum of 10s upon every ton of ore shipped from any port in Namaqualand.[39] Provision was also made for the re-appropriation of the ground if, after three years, less than 50 tons of ore had been shipped.[40] The whole question of royalties and the difficulties in connection with ensuring its payment resulted in a drawn-out correspondence with the Government, which was only finally resolved when The Cape Copper Mining Company undertook to pay the salary of a customs officer at Port Nolloth.

The settlement of the lease question and the influx of miners following the opening up of Namaqualand affected the indigenous population somewhat adversely. We shall only briefly consider some of the social implications of the settlement of the lease question.

The Surveyor-General, Charles Bell, considered the question of 'natives' rights a most important one, and felt that they should be secured against encroachment by Whites upon land which they had beneficially occupied before the annexation of the territory. He did not, however, consider that they had any right to claim mineral rights to such land. In an attempt to rationalize the Government's attitude on the matter, he stated:

I said, 'it appeared to me that copper was one of the Creator's gifts to man, and that their country, although poor in other respects, was rich in that metal; while in many portions of the earth, otherwise rich, nations had need of it, and would gladly send food and clothing, and tools and money, to Namaqualand, in exchange for it. I spoke of the skill, and labour, and expense they saw bestowed on the few mines opened, and asked them if they were fit to open all the mines, so as to offer to exchange their produce with the rest of the world, or whether they could smelt and work up and use the copper themselves. The reply usually was "No, no; take the copper, we can't raise it, and don't want it." I then further said all that the Government appears to me to have done, has been to prevent quarrelling and oppression, by saying that no one shall dig for copper without leave, and by giving, to such men as will honestly pay for what damage they may do, leave to dig copper ore; nothing more. Every blade of grass, every drop of water, taken by the copper-diggers, from any one, must be paid for; and all that can be demanded of you is, that you shall not refuse to sell water and grass where necessary, for a fair price, if possible, because captious objections and extortionate demands, if permitted, would effectually keep the ore in the ground, as at present, useless to mankind in general. You say you apprehend oppression; rest quiet; – I cannot conceive why the Government should oppress you more than other men; but take care you do not oppress yourselves. Are the present prices you receive for labour, for carriage of ore, and for your crops, symptomatic of oppression? I think not; but your waste of these prices, formerly unheard of, in folly and vice, to the destruction of yourselves and your oxen, is an oppression from which no Government can effectually shield you. And if, hereafter, your sons have difficulty in finding healthy and respectable wives of their own race, you will recollect, with bitterness, the drink, food, clothing, or indifference that induced you to shut your eyes while your daughters tempted the crowds of single men now landing on your coast. The Government cannot protect men who will not protect themselves in these respects, and struggle against the great oppressors of this land, namely, idleness and improvidence. You, yourselves, see, and no sensible man can avoid seeing, that a great change is taking place here; and while, as a friend of your race, I may congratulate the industrious and the prudent among you, on your improved prospects under that change, I warn you that the idler and the drunkard must give place by the force of circimstances which no Government can control.'[41]

What the more callous epoch of *laissez-faire* saw as the sins of weakness of the individual, we now know to be the social ills universally attendant upon the disruption of tribal societies by industrialization. But while we may differently attribute the causes, as a prophesy, Charles Bell's prediction stands the test of time.

One of the chief reasons for Brecher's claims to the mineral rights of the mission station was probably the fact that, under mission control, the sale of strong drink could be outlawed, as it was under the agreement entered into between The Namaqua Mining Company and the Office Bearers of Steinkopf.[42] The Civil Commissioner of Namaqualand in 1872 was of the opinion that the 'very free' sale of liquor in mining districts such as Namaqualand should be prohibited by special enactment. He considered that there was no doubt that before the working of the mines the indigenous population had been 'well-to-do', but that since the introduction of brandy they had been 'completely ruined'.[43]

In the 1860s it appears that the dual effects of drought and loss of cattle through copper-riding[44] had so impoverished the indigenous population that they were reduced to committing crimes in order to go to prison where they were fed by the Government. This practice led the Civil Commissioner of Namaqualand in 1866 to comment upon three possible alternative ways of reducing crime; the first of which would be to utilize convicts in road-construction (which he considered preventive rather than curative); the second, the sale of Crown Lands and the encouragement of mining enterprise which would open up employment; and the third, a reduction of the rations of the convicts of which he says:

The plan of reducing the rations of the convicts is at once the most effectual and the most just punishment. It is really a more severe and a less brutalizing punishment than the lash, and has not the tendency attributed to the latter of ensuring a man's return for a second infliction, while it is the cheapest for those who have to bear both the loss of the theft and their share of the cost of punishing the thieves.[45]

The nature of the country forced the people to be largely nomadic. The result was that the civilizing influences of the mission and its school could only reach them intermittently. Nevertheless all the evidence seems to indicate that until the 'days of copper, canteens and contact with Europeans', the Namaqua/Coloured made appreciable progress under guidance of the missionaries. They came to own fair numbers of large and small stock and learned to work the soil on a fairly large scale, taking into account the nature of the land.[46] Unfortunately the lure of easy money by riding copper, and its concomitant drinking sessions, resulted in the neglect of agriculture. The acquisition of wagons which became redundant after the construction of The Cape Copper Mining Company's railway was a less profitable long-term investment than might have been made by investment in agricultural implements. The vesting of the mineral rights to the stations in the state cut off any possibility of the development of a 'native' mining enterprise.[47]

NOTES TO CHAPTER 3

1 J. A. Heese, *Onderwys in die Geskiedenis van Namaqualand*, p. 20 and also pp. 39-40
2 G.8 – '55, p. 3
3 J. A. Heese, op cit, p. 25
4 The boundary had been extended to the Kousie River in 1805
5 J. E. Alexander, op cit, vol. I p. 35
6 R.L.R. 24, p. 108
7 S.C.5 – '56, p. 32, Col-Sec. to Rev. Brecher, 14/9/1842
8 W. van Reenen in his journal (1792) mentioned a certain Guilliam Visage who had a farm at the present Keetmanshoop, see *The Journal of Jacob Wikar (1779)* and *The Journals of Jacobus Coetsé Jansz (1760)*: and *Willem van Reenen (1791)*, (Cape Town, van Riebeeck Society 1935), pp. 306-307
9 S.C.5 – '56, p. 49, memorial from F. Brecher to Cathcart, 10/12/1853
10 Ibid, p. 37
11 A memorial had been addressed to the Government early in 1850, but as upon enquiry no trace of this could be found, the Government requested a copy of said memorial
12 S.C.5 – '56, p. 48, memorial from F. Brecher to Sir H. G. Smith, Jan 1851
13 Ibid, p. 49, Col-Sec. to Rev. Brecher, 29/9/1851
14 Messrs von Schlicht, Stoll, Thomson, Watson & Co., and Prince, Collison & Co
15 G.8 – '54, p. 1, Thomson, Watson & Co. to Actg Col-Sec., 6/4/1853
16 Ibid, p. 1, Actg Col-Sec. to Messrs Thomson, Watson & Co., 12/4/1853
17 Ibid, pp. 3-4
18 Ibid, p. 3
19 S.C.5 – '56, pp. 34-35, Rev. Brecher to Messrs A. von Schlicht and G. Prince, 17/11/1853
20 Ibid, p. 34, agreement between members of the Mission Station of Steinkopf and Messrs Stoll, von Schlicht, Prince, Collison & Co., and Thomson, Watson & Co., dated 9/11/1853

21 The Lieut-Governor
22 S.C.5 – '56, p. 39
23 Ibid, p. 36, Thomson, Watson & Co. to Actg Col-Sec., 14/12/1853
24 Ibid, pp. 36-37, Actg Col-Sec. to Thomson, Watson & Co., 19/12/1853
25 Ibid, p. 51, Actg Col-Sec. to Rev. Brecher, 31/12/1853
26 Ibid, p. 38, memorial of Captain, Commandant, etc., to Sir G. Cathcart, 30/1/854
27 Ibid, p. 52, agreement between Namaqua Mining Co. and Office Bearers of Steinkopf, 30/1/1854
28 A 'Ticket of Occupation' was issued for Steinkopf on 9/12/1874, 27 years after the extension of the boundary.
Cl. VII reserved to the Government or its agents, all mineral rights
29 W. P. Carstens, *The Structure of a Cape Coloured Reserve*, (Cape Town, Oxford University Press 1966), p. 30
30 S.C.2 – '55, p. 16. It was hoped to use this income for the appointment of a geological surveyor
31 The exact number of leases granted is not positively known
32 *The Cape Monitor*, 27/10/1855
33 S.C.5 – '64, p. v
34 S.C.5 – '56, p. iii
35 The No. 6 Mining Company, 18 tons, and The Cape of Good Hope Mining Company, 15 tons
36 See G.8 – '54, pp. 38-39, and p. 41; and S.C.2 – '55, pp. 14-15
37 The Western Province Mining Company, for example, out of a total expenditure of £5 172, had paid £35 as rental (or rather deposit) for the 14 centres they had leased. The Cameron Mining Company, out of a total expenditure of £3 000 had paid only £43 15s as deposit on 175 morgen leased by them
38 S.C.5 – '64, p. vi
39 *Act No. 12 of 1865*, Cl. IV
40 Ibid, Cl. XIII
41 G.8 – '55, pp. 6-7
42 S.C.5 – '56, p. 34
43 *Cape Blue Book* 1872. Report of the Civil Commissioner of Namaqualand, JJ-4
44 See pp. 84-85
45 *Cape Blue Book* 1866. Report of the Civil Commissioner of Namaqualand, JJ-47. A similar conclusion was reached by the *Select Committee on Thefts of Livestock*, A3 – '63, pp. iii-iv
46 J. S. Marais, *The Cape Coloured People 1652-1937*, (London, Longmans, Green 1939), p. 76
47 Thus, for instance, preventing people from being able to develop more extensively the practice of 'tributing', because of the fear of White competition. See W. P. Carstens, op cit, pp. 54-55

Chapter 4

The greatest single problem affecting the profitable exploitation of Namaqualand's mineral deposits has been, and continues to be to this day, the distance of these deposits from a market. So, although the existence of these deposits had been known from the earliest days of the settlement at the Cape, it was only when Phillips & King realized just how rich the deposits were that their commercial exploitation began. The first 11 tons of ore were exported by Phillips & King aboard the steamer *Bosphorus* on August 31, 1852.[1] Transport in the immediate future became even more difficult to obtain for, while each shipment received in Cape Town affected the value of the shares of the company shipping the ore, the companies engaged in fierce competition for the limited amount of transport, sending costs up to ridiculous levels.[2]

During the speculative mania of 1854/55 there was a great deal of talk about the possibility of constructing a railway line or tramway,[3] though this never bore fruit. Memorialists complained that the greatest obstacle to their raising the capital necessary for railway construction lay in the shortness of the lease period.[4] It is more likely that their desire for an extension of the lease period was motivated not so much with a view to construction of a line of railway as by the hope of profitable sale of the leases to overseas capitalists.[5]

The Government, however, turned a deaf ear to the entreaties of memorialists who petitioned for an extension of the lease period, or the sale of the centres as freehold, or the construction of a line of railway by the Government itself, and this despite the recommendations of two Select Committees appointed to enquire into the practicability of introducing railway communication into the Colony.[6] The Government's decision against the rendering of any assistance was founded on the belief that, notwithstanding all the disadvantages lessees suffered, they were nevertheless able to dispose of their ores in England for between £30 to £40 per ton, while it cost them only about £13 per ton to get it there.[7]

The first of these Select Committees was set up in 1854. In their report they distinguished between two cases – ordinary cases and 'extraordinary' cases. In ordinary cases, it was suggested that the Government should only endorse a sub-guarantee. In the case of Namaqualand, however, it was considered that the '...recent discovery of valuable and extensive deposits...(of copper ore)...has opened up a field for successful railway speculation, such as South Africa has never before presented'.[8] As a consequence the Committee announced that the benefit to the whole Colony from the development of a successful mining enterprise was of sufficient importance to warrant '...rendering such reasonable aid as may be required to accomplish the completion of Railroad communication from the sea-coast to a central position in the Copper Mining Districts'.[9] No indication was however given as to what form such 'reasonable aid' might take. A further Select Committee was appointed in 1855 to determine this.

The Select Committee of 1855 found that there existed '...immense quantities of copper ore, of excellent quality,...which can be raised to the surface at a comparatively trifling cost'.[10] With the existing means of transport, however, only ore containing more than 25% of pure copper could be exported profitably. Since the ore was found, on the whole, to vary in richness from 12% to 18%, unless something was done to improve the existing means of transport, many of the lessees would be compelled to abandon their workings.[11] The Committee suggested that three courses of action were open to the Government, viz., an extension of the lease period from 15 to 50 years, the guarantee of a reasonable rate of interest upon capital advanced for such a project, or the Colonial Government itself taking an interest in the construction of a line of rail. The Committee, while they would have been pleased to see any of these courses followed, felt that on account of the state of the Colonial finances, an extension in the lease period would be the most practical, since this would place the lessees in a favourable position for making the necessary improvements to the roads without any cost to the Government. Furthermore, they pointed out that such improvements would increase the value of ungranted Crown land at no cost to the Government.[12] In any event, none of these courses was adopted. This was probably due to a combination of factors; firstly, the collapse of the copper mining mania, and secondly, the recommendations of the Surveyor-General, Charles Bell, who advised against an extension of the lease period or the pledging of any part of the Colonial revenue for a speculation of this nature.

Bell favoured meeting the expense of facilitating access to the mines by a servitude on the enhanced value of the mine when it reverted to the Government. He recognized that, in the case of roads and railways common to particular localities, there would be enormous practical difficulties, but nevertheless suggested that some means might be found whereby mine and railway shares could be sold simultaneously, and that at the end of the lease period arbitrators might settle the question of purchase money for the benefit of the outgoing lessee.[13] That nothing came of all this was largely due to the fact that the companies themselves had very little money for investment in a railway or tramway, since most of them had invested their entire capital in securing, and attempting to work, enormous numbers of centres.

The Select Committee of 1855 had also reported that the construction of good common roads should be undertaken and suggested that convict labour might be used for this purpose. At that time, there were three classes of roads in the Colony: main roads, divisional roads and other public roads. The main roads were proclaimed and constructed by the Government, but kept in repair by the divisional councils. The divisional roads were proclaimed, constructed and kept in repair by the divisional councils. Other public roads were sometimes repaired by the divisional councils but they were not legally responsible for them.[14] Since the Government did not proclaim a main road, and Namaqualand had no divisional council until 1861, the roads in Namaqualand fell into the category of 'other public roads'. Because the roads required repair at the end of each riding season – the average duration of which was about four to five months,[15] Phillips & King, in their private capacity and at their own expense, were reduced to employing gangs of labourers for the purpose of keeping the roads in some sort of repair. Of this state of affairs, Andrew Wyley, the Geological-Surveyor, commented that the entire onus of keeping the roads in repair should not be thrown upon the mining proprietors. To back up this argument, he pointed out that about £40 000 per annum was expended upon wages, transport and stores, most of this within the Colony. To his way of thinking, this was proof that the state of the roads was not simply a private affair – the mines having done more to enrich the Colony than their owners. Since the very existence of these mines depended upon the state of the roads, he felt that a small annual subsidy to keep the roads in a passable state was not an unreasonable request.[16]

About a year before Wyley's statement, J. S. Rivers, the Civil Commissioner of Namaqualand, had written a report to the Government concerning the appalling state of the two main roads used for export, viz., one to Hondeklip Bay and the other to Port Nolloth.[17] In the interim, though, nothing had been done.

The most frequently used vehicle was the light Cape wagon drawn by ten mules, although, especially in good seasons, the heavier ox-wagon was fairly common. The former means of transport was very much more expensive than the latter. The normal load was supposed to be 3 000 lbs., but because of the bad roads, by the time the wagons reached the coast, they seldom contained more than 2 000 lbs. Ore was transported in bags but these tended to chafe through as a result of all the heavy wear and tear.

Experiments were at one time made using Scotch carts, but these were of no avail.[18] Andrew Wyley even suggested the introduction of camels, but the expense and difficulty involved in importing a large enough number with which to experiment deterred the mining proprietors.[19] This, incidentally, was not the first time it had been suggested that camels might be used for transporting copper ore. Commissioner de Mist in his *Memorandum on the Cape* in 1802 had stated that:

> If the sea is too far distant, and it is found necessary to transport the copper to Cape Town by road, it would be far better to import and breed camels at the Cape, and use them instead of draught oxen, since the camel will be far more at home in that region, resembling as it does the desert plains in the north of Africa. In addition, the camelopard, whose habitat is in the vicinity of the mines, is not unlike the camel, which we think could be used with success, and would be bound to benefit trade with the interior.[20]

No one has as yet attempted to employ the giraffe as a beast of burden.

Not only was carriage difficult to obtain, limited as it was by the state of the veld, but in addition its cost was exorbitant. It was claimed by certain petitioners with regard to the construction of a railway in 1855 that the total cost for carriage alone per ton of ore from the mines to the smelting works at Swansea was about £16. This was made up of charges from the mines to the coast of £7 10s and £3 for back-carriage, with or without goods. The freight from there to Table Bay was £1 10s and from there to London £2 to £3, from London to the smelting works at Swansea about 10s to 15s per ton.[21] The cost of carriage to the coast was, in fact, almost equal to the overall costs of mining.[22] The real problem was the sandy belt stretching inland from the coast, the average cost per ton mile through this area being three to four times as much as that on the rest of the road.[23]

Phillips & King, in order to ensure the transport of their ores to the coast, systematically bought up almost all the farms on route to Hondeklip Bay. This also put them in a position where they could 'starve' out their only serious rivals, The Namaqua Mining Company. In 1855, John Blades Currey was appointed as manager of the latter concern specifically to try and organize the transport of their ore to the coast. This he was able to accomplish by obtaining outspan rights on the farm Kookfontein, owned by a certain Jan Agenbag, although Agenbag refused to enter into a written contract.[24]

As may be seen from Table A (p. 127) exports of copper ore rose rapidly over the years 1852 to 1862. By 1860 copper had become the Colony's second most important export. Nevertheless, exports of wool were so much greater and Namaqualand so isolated from the rest of the Colony that copper certainly cannot be said to have had a very large influence upon the development of the Colony.[25]

The death of two of the partners in the firm of Phillips & King in 1862 compelled the disposal of their property in Namaqualand. A large interest in The Cape of Good Hope Copper Mining Company, Limited,[26] which took over their mines was however, retained by individual members of the house. John King was appointed a director of The Cape Copper Mining Company. In addition the firm of King & Sons acted as managers of the company's affairs in the Cape.

In the prospectus of The Cape Copper Mining Company, which was formed by John Taylor & Sons of London in 1862 with a capital of £150 000 in 15 000 shares of £10 each, attention was drawn to the benefits likely to be derived from the application of capital; firstly by concentrating the ores before shipment; and secondly by constructing a line of rail or tramway over the worst portion of the road to the coast. It was stated in the prospectus that:

> The results which have already been obtained prove that the deposits of ore must be very large and unusually rich; for, not only have 19 000 tons been sent home of the best kinds, and have been sold for more than £500 000, but these ores have been picked out from vast quantities of lower quality, amounting it is believed, to nearly 50 000 tons, which are lying in heaps at the mines, containing from 5 up to 18 per cent of Copper.
>
> The transport of the ores to the Coast has been a difficulty of no small magnitude especially in the commencement of operations. Bad roads, a tract of flat deep sand, rude wagons, a want of trained oxen and of pasturage, have all tended to render the carriage both tedious and costly.
>
> In undertaking the technical management of this concern, we have in view the advantages which may be derived from the application of capital in several ways.
>
> By the introduction of some of the best modes of concentrating the poorer ores, both by dressing and by smelting into a regulus, largely increased returns may be secured, and a considerable reduction in the current cost of raising the richer ores will be effected.

Again, to remedy the difficulties, and to lessen the cost of transport of the ores to the coast, the state of the roads must be improved, and instead of employing oxen and mules to drag the loaded wagons a distance of 15 miles over the deep sandy flat...causing them to suffer more from want of herbage and good water in this length, than over the whole of the rest of the road, we have recommended that a tramway, to be worked by horses over this portion of the road, shall be laid down.

We estimate that £18 000 will pay the whole cost of the rails, spikes and sleepers, and of sending them out from this country, also of forming and laying the road, as well as of wagons suitable for the carriage of ore and coals. The effect of this tramway will be not only largely to diminish the cost of carrying, but it will liberate, as it were, many oxen and mules, and allow them to make more journeys than they now do, both working cheaper and carrying a larger quantity down annually.[27]

The purchase consideration for the property of Messrs Phillips & King in Namaqualand was some £73 000,[28] including £30 000 in paid-up shares. Phillips & King had certainly done well out of their investment in Namaqualand, for the mines had yielded from 1853 until October 1862 ore to the value of £515 752, producing a profit of more than £115 000.[29]

The formation of The Cape Copper Mining Company ushered in a new era in Namaqualand's history. It also advanced plans making profitable ores which contained below 16%.[30]

Springbok

In 1852 when operations by Phillips & King began in earnest, Springbokfontein consisted of one mud cabin and a few mat huts.[1] By 1854 A. G. Bain noted that the nucleus of a rapidly rising village already existed.[2] The growth of the village was directly related to the opening up of the mine, so that by 1857 when operations were well under way, Springbokfontein had already become a large mining station with substantial buildings such as officers' and workmen's houses, mess rooms, stores, wagon-makers' and blacksmiths' shops, stables, forage stores; and scattered about were to be found all the amenities necessary for an extensive mine. There was also a post office, a small church, and a prison, '...a thing not altogether to be dispensed with, even in the best regulated communities'.[3] As in any mining camp the prison was a very necessary requirement. In 1855, the newly appointed Resident

Magistrate, Josiah Rivers, had requested, in the absence of a gaol, the purchase of a set of stocks for the detainment of prisoners.[4] After the construction of the prison it seems to have been kept fairly full.[5]

The mining population was a fairly mixed bunch, but was predominantly Coloured. Andrew Wyley in his report on Namaqualand described the labouring population:

> The mining population of Namaqualand, including those employed in transport, consists chiefly of artisans and labourers from the Cape and adjoining districts – a very miscellaneous assemblage. Tradesmen of all sorts, soldiers and sailors, farm labourers, quarrymen, may all be found at work in the mines. There are few real miners, and from the method of mining carried on here, they are seldom required.
>
> In Springbokfontein and Spectaakle much of the work is done, and pretty well done, by coloured people, from various parts of the colony. There is less trouble in managing these than the white workmen, who are not, as may be supposed, always of the best and most tractable character, and between whom and the various managing officers misunderstandings are pretty certain to take place, – especially when the former have succeeded in smuggling up an anker or two of brandy from Hondeklip Bay, an article which, beyond the daily allowance, is strictly prohibited. On these occasions disgraceful scenes sometimes occur, but they are not at all common.[6]

That such scenes were not common must almost certainly have been the result of a pact entered into between John Wild, as manager of Phillips & King's interests, and John Blades Currey, as manager of The Namaqua Mining Company, that neither would engage a man discharged by the other. And when the men discovered that to be discharged

> ...meant to be turned adrift and having to foot it for 70 miles through an almost waterless desert to reach the coast and that even when they got there, the Company's chartered vessels would not take them on board they soon came to their senses and there was peace at the mines.[7]

Besides, as Wyley pointed out:

> The presence of a magistrate, and a prison near at hand, act as a salutary check upon the more riotously disposed on these occasions.[8]

The choice of Springbokfontein as the seat of magistracy in 1855 had been made through the offer of accommodation and provision of supplies by Phillips & King, and, were it not for this, the village would soon have become deserted since the mine was worked out within a few years. E. A. Judge, who arrived in 1861, in order to take up the post of Relieving Resident Magistrate from Anthing who was engaged upon a tour of the northern districts, described the village:

I found there was a small hotel there at which I was able to put up. It was a long low building with no second floor. In fact there was not a single two storeyed building in the place, nor were there more than about 20 separate buildings altogether...It was the headquarters of the Copper Company and was not much more than a mining camp. There was a copper mine which was worked from a drive into one of the hills at the back of the village, but this mine was nearly worked out and was abandoned not long afterwards.

...Springbok was a very small village. I don't think the inhabitants numbered more than 100 persons. The Copper Co's staff consisted of a manager and 3 or 4 clerks and a few miners, none of them with their wives, then there was a doctor and his wife with a family of small children, there were two shops giving employment to perhaps 8 or 10 persons and a small hotel accommodating not more than about 14 people including servants. There was no church and no clergyman of any denomination. My own staff consisted of one clerk and a chief constable and a gaoler and 4 or 5 coloured constables. There were besides a few bastards and hottentots who lived in huts made of old sacks.[9]

Only shortly before the arrival of Judge, Anthing had engaged in an extensive correspondence concerning the removal of the seat of magistracy from Springbokfontein. He advised removal because in his estimation there was not sufficient water to meet the requirements of the village but, even if there were, he considered that Springbokfontein was not the most suitable site for a permanent seat of magistracy. The reason for this was the position of the magistrate vis à vis Phillips & King, a position which Anthing considered neither dignified nor independent.[10] The Magistrate was dependent upon the Company for his every requirement. Furthermore, since the village was a private and not a public one, only those people of whom Phillips & King approved could remain overnight as all accommodation was supplied by the Company.[11]

Apparently:

Parties having business to transact at the court, if they are not liked by the manager are not allowed to remain on the place. They may not tarry. They can receive no shelter, no refreshments for man or beast. They must be off, it matters not at what amount of inconvenience. There is no place in the vicinity where such parties can go for accommodation. The consequence is that frequently people have been put to the greatest possible inconvenience. I know of instances in which parties after riding long distances to transact business at the court have been obliged to ride back under a burning sun, their horses and themselves literally knocked up from want of refreshment and shelter.[12]

One result of this sort of attitude was that people were not able to enjoy the benefit of a district surgeon because they were unable to remain in Springbokfontein for the doctor's continued attendance. Also, as Anthing noted, there were few women in residence at Spring-

Fig. 9 Springbokfontein reduction works c1870 (H. R. Moffatt Collection, South African Library, Cape Town)

Fig. 10 Springbok c1880 (J. F. Goch Album, South African Library, Cape Town)

Fig. 11 Springbok c1880 (from the private collection of H. R. Moffatt, Cape Town)

Fig. 12 Hondeklip Bay 1854 (from a sketchbook in the Library of Parliament, Cape Town)

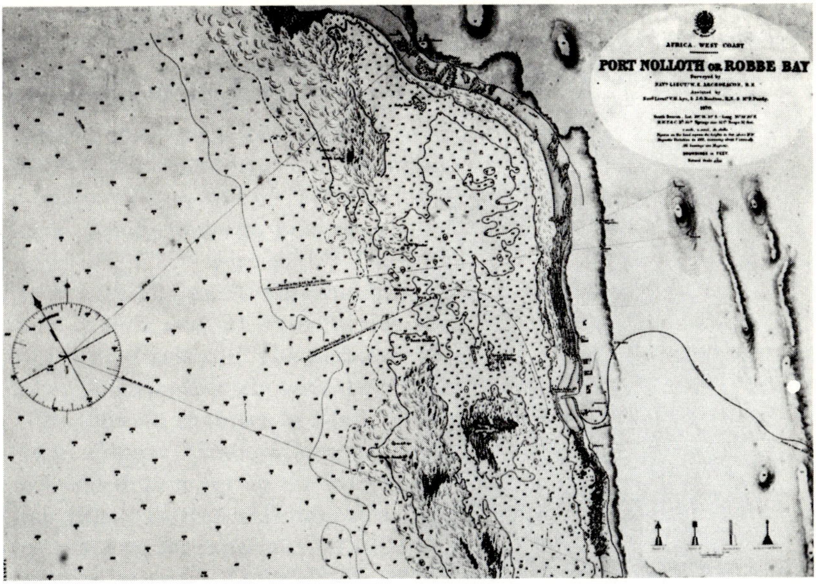

Fig. 13 Port Nolloth (Cape Archives M2/890)

Fig. 14 *Rol-vaatjie*, Port Nolloth (from the private collection of H. R. Moffatt, Cape Town)

such an exclusive attitude by their successors in respect of their new headquarters.

However, 1881 saw a reduction in shipping costs, and the consequent re-opening of the Springbokfontein mine.[25] At first the mine showed excellent prospects of improving, and a great deal of work was done by The Cape Copper Mining Company in repairing many of their old houses, etc.[26] Work was still being carried on in 1883,[27] but with how much success it is difficult to assess. It is also difficult to say exactly when work stopped once more – it was reported in 1889 that the workings at Springbok had increased.[28] By 1886, when W. C. Scully arrived to take up his position as Relieving Resident Magistrate, he found an attractive village of some 200 inhabitants.[29] But, if Scully found the village attractive on first view, he was soon to discover an undercurrent of fear and hatred.

Springbokfontein, he shortly discovered, had been terrorised for some time by the local gaoler, a certain William Genricks, who was subsequently charged with both the crimes of murder and indecent assault. In his inimitable style Scully described the situation:

> ...for some time the doings of Genricks have been a scandal to the community, and the peaceable inhabitants of this place have had to submit to the most odious and galling tyranny on the part of this man. No one man or woman – dare venture anywhere near the gaol for fear of being insulted in the grossest manner by this brute. He was only on speaking terms with two people in the whole place, and no one else could pass the gaol without being yelled at by him, or by a tame lunatic that is confined in the gaol and that he trained to shout at women and others – He has been seen crouching behind his wall, whilst all the prisoners yelled and jeered at a lady (a Mrs Loynes) going to her W.C. which was in sight of the gaol. This W.C. had to be moved away to where it could not be seen from the gaol, on this account...were it not for the horrible things that took place inside the prison, and the slow miseries inflicted upon these poor sick prisoners, this would be a funny business. The idea of a village being domineered over by a man in the position of a gaoler is excessively comical. It shows what *can* happen, and how truth is often stranger than fiction.[30]

Scully's patrician nature seemed to be rather upset at the idea of anyone in the lowly position of a gaoler domineering an entire village, but in many ways who is in a better position to dominate a group of people than a gaoler? But if the inhabitants of Springbokfontein were afraid of Genricks, the prisoners must have been completely terrified, conditions in the gaol being appalling. The cells were extremely crowded, and a great deal of trouble was experienced with bugs. These tiny creatures, it seems, were an absolute menace:

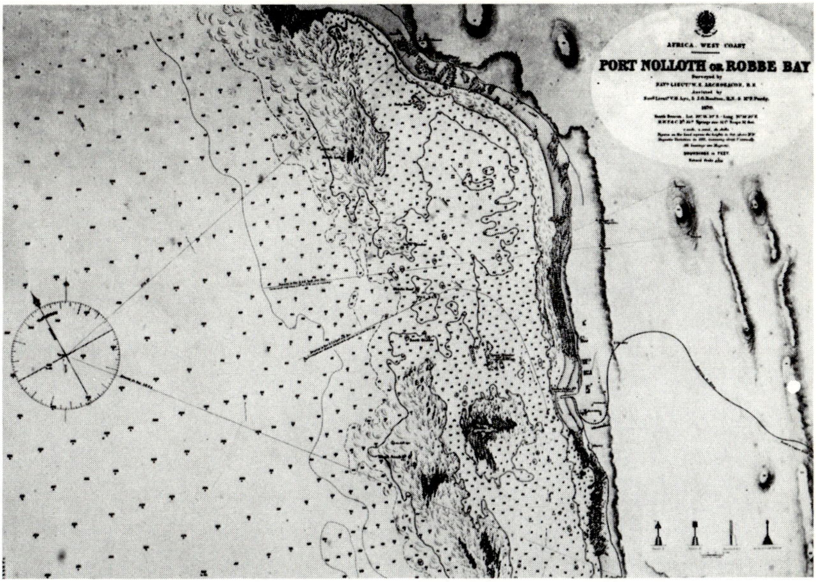

Fig. 13 Port Nolloth (Cape Archives M2/890)

Fig. 14 *Rol-vaatjie*, Port Nolloth (from the private collection of H. R. Moffatt, Cape Town)

Fig. 15 'Basket' used for raising passengers to the pier at Port Nolloth (from the private collection of H. R. Moffatt, Cape Town)

Fig. 16 Port Nolloth Civic Centre, looking North c1905 (H. R. Moffatt Collection, South African Library, Cape Town)

bokfontein, since the Company had '. . .set their faces against married men settling'.[13] Thus, although the community was in urgent need of an attorney, a secretary for the Divisional Council, and a surveyor, none could be found who were bachelors, and the district had to do without these men, and without any 'additions to refined society'.[14] But in fact the magistracy was not moved. Instead it was decided to create a public village, and in 1862 Patrick Fletcher, a surveyor, laid out the town. An auction was held on October 28, 1862, when plots to the value of £6 260 were sold.[15] The creation of a public village allowed for the establishment of a church, and in 1866 the first clergyman, one Rev. Morris, arrived. Prior to this Judge had read Matins in the Court Room on Sundays.[16] The mid-sixties saw the growth of a lively social life in Springbokfontein with the holding of race meetings[17] and balls.[18]

In 1864 an engineer, a Mr J. F. Davis who was employed by The Cape Copper Mining Company, arrived in Namaqualand. It was to be his duty to set up the works necessary for smelting the ore which was then to be sent to Britain as a regulus.[19] By 1866 smelting was taking place on an experimental scale, and the value of ore smelted during that year was £2 096.[20] By 1867 the Springbokfontein Reduction Works was fully operational and regulus to the value of £15 298 was produced.[21] This plant was to have only a short life, being soon superseded by the O'okiep Reduction Works which came into operation in 1870. By 1872 there were only a few men working the Springbokfontein mine. The village was nevertheless considered an important one, with its public offices, pretty English Church, and substantial houses.[22] In 1875 the population totalled 244, and there were 25 houses and 20 huts and tents.[23] However, the removal of the headquarters of The Cape Copper Mining Company to O'okiep and the closing down of the mine at Springbokfontein, caused the village to become virtually deserted by 1877, and a traveller through Namaqualand found Springbokfontein

> . . .now nearly deserted. A few shopkeepers, and the magistrate with his clerk and the few constables and a wagon-maker, form the whole white population; and even these would not be in existence were it not that O'okiep, being the private property of The Cape Copper Mining Company, is not open to the public. The village looks as if it had undergone a siege; everwhere are falling walls, – roofs, doors and windows have all vanished, carried away by the remorseless hands of carpenters to form part of new buildings at the new mine in O'okiep.[24]

Thus if Springbokfontein had once suffered because of the exclusive attitude of Phillips & King, its survival seems to have been due to just such an exclusive attitude by their successors in respect of their new headquarters.

However, 1881 saw a reduction in shipping costs, and the consequent re-opening of the Springbokfontein mine.[25] At first the mine showed excellent prospects of improving, and a great deal of work was done by The Cape Copper Mining Company in repairing many of their old houses, etc.[26] Work was still being carried on in 1883,[27] but with how much success it is difficult to assess. It is also difficult to say exactly when work stopped once more – it was reported in 1889 that the workings at Springbok had increased.[28] By 1886, when W. C. Scully arrived to take up his position as Relieving Resident Magistrate, he found an attractive village of some 200 inhabitants.[29] But, if Scully found the village attractive on first view, he was soon to discover an undercurrent of fear and hatred.

Springbokfontein, he shortly discovered, had been terrorised for some time by the local gaoler, a certain William Genricks, who was subsequently charged with both the crimes of murder and indecent assault. In his inimitable style Scully described the situation:

> ...for some time the doings of Genricks have been a scandal to the community, and the peaceable inhabitants of this place have had to submit to the most odious and galling tyranny on the part of this man. No one man or woman – dare venture anywhere near the gaol for fear of being insulted in the grossest manner by this brute. He was only on speaking terms with two people in the whole place, and no one else could pass the gaol without being yelled at by him, or by a tame lunatic that is confined in the gaol and that he trained to shout at women and others – He has been seen crouching behind his wall, whilst all the prisoners yelled and jeered at a lady (a Mrs Loynes) going to her W.C. which was in sight of the gaol. This W.C. had to be moved away to where it could not be seen from the gaol, on this account...were it not for the horrible things that took place inside the prison, and the slow miseries inflicted upon these poor sick prisoners, this would be a funny business. The idea of a village being domineered over by a man in the position of a gaoler is excessively comical. It shows what *can* happen, and how truth is often stranger than fiction.[30]

Scully's patrician nature seemed to be rather upset at the idea of anyone in the lowly position of a gaoler domineering an entire village, but in many ways who is in a better position to dominate a group of people than a gaoler? But if the inhabitants of Springbokfontein were afraid of Genricks, the prisoners must have been completely terrified, conditions in the gaol being appalling. The cells were extremely crowded, and a great deal of trouble was experienced with bugs. These tiny creatures, it seems, were an absolute menace:

The bugs are phenomenal in number, appetite and activity, and consequently the human inmates of the gaol have a lively time of it. The other night at 10.30 I went down to the gaol and found an awful state of things. The bugs were falling down in a constant shower from the ceiling, and marching down the walls in companies, regiments and brigades. In the corners they covered the walls completely. Next morning I went down again, and there they were, crawling up the walls home again in various stages of repletion. I have taken it upon myself to invest in a quantity of insect destroying powder, and shall endeavour to get some 'Dagga' hemp... to smoke them out with.[31]

Genricks who had meanwhile been imprisoned, turned pious:

As is usual with ruffians of his stamp, Mr Genricks has turned pious. He says he knows that the word of the Lord is stretched over him etc., etc., etc., and all that sort of clap trap, and in fact to hear him talk, one would think that a special picket of angels was encamped over his cell. I always think of 'Uriah Heep' whenever I see him.[32]

Genricks was eventually found not guilty of the crime of murder, and received only a light sentence for the grievous crime of assault, which he, together with 'his tame lunatic', had perpetrated upon the unfortunate Sannah Bok, some time an inmate of the Springbokfontein gaol.[33] Actually Scully hoped to put the prisoners to better use than had hitherto been the case – he intended following the example set in Kimberley with regard to the De Beers Mining Company – and hire out convicts to The Cape Copper Mining Company to work their Springbokfontein mine.[34] However, in the absence of such an arrangement, and hence the only possible remunerative employment, and taking into account the lack of a village management board,[35] convicts were used upon the following works; firstly, the repair and maintenance of the streets and roads of the village; secondly, clearing up rubbish; thirdly, planting and watering trees in the streets and recreation grounds; fourthly, the repair and maintenance of public recreation grounds; and fifthly, cleaning public wells and dams.[36] Convicts were also used to keep the village supplied with fresh water at a rate of 6d per barrel.[37] Some difficulty in obtaining sufficient prisoners was experienced however, and it was suggested that prisoners serving longer sentences be kept in Springbok in order to meet the demand for their services.[38]

A greater tyrant though, and certainly one which could wield its power with almost total impunity, was The Cape Copper Mining Company, more especially as it was represented in the form of its 'Super'. Scully commented upon this as well:

The whole Namaqualand system of local management was arranged on the basis of no one having any rights, (for) with the exception of the air one breathed, no necessity of existence could be obtained except by special grace of the preposterous person... (the Company's Superintendent)...who wielded the Copper Sceptre like a rod of iron.[39]

No pleasure was too small to escape this tyrant's eye, and no pleasure could be enjoyed without his special permission:

The Cape Copper Company practically owned the bodies, and consequently tyrannized over the souls of its inhabitants. The local head of the Company was, except in the matter of mining, quite uneducated. He was as pompous as a grocer-alderman and as touchy as a cuttle-fish. It was not alone that one had to give him precedence in everything – that I have never objected to doing; but he expected you to approach him with abject homage – to crawl on the ground before his hobnailed feet. If one could imagine a Baron of the Middle Ages with tyrannical tendencies, a navvy, and a beadle all rolled into one, one might begin to realise 'The Super', as he was termed. But without experiencing it, you could never realise what it meant to be under the heavy, callous thumb of such a being.

'The Super' was, as a matter of fact, as much an autocrat in his little sphere as is the Tsar in All the Russias. The Company, of which he was practically the irresponsible executive, owned the house I lived in, the court-room in which I sat as magistrate, the gaol in which the prisoners I sentenced were confined, and the well from which was drawn the only water available for my household.[40]

One must admit, however, that Scully always seemed to have to deal with the most objectionable characters. Thus in 1891, for instance, he complained of his chief constable, a certain W. A. N. Musgrave:

Mr Musgrave possesses in a very high degree the faculty of being very offensive without committing himself in any definite way, and the manner in which he accomplishes his purpose is difficult to describe. For instance, he makes elaborate military salutes whenever he sees me, intones his voice to unnatural pitches, makes unnecessary and trivial requests in stilled periods of mock politeness and enters my office from time to time with a peculiar gait which can best be described as a sort of subdued prance, or a hybrid between the professional mince of a dancing master and the swagger of a stage dragoon.

The antics alluded to must however be seen to be appreciated. Under the circumstances it must be obvious that Mr Musgrave will have to go from here...as although perfectly harmless in itself his ridiculous and insubordinate conduct may have a very bad effect upon the morale of the Department.[41]

The great difficulty was that people were simply not prepared to go to Namaqualand, and so anyone who was willing was sent.

In 1895 Namaqualand experienced such a severe drought that several baboons visited Springbokfontein in order to obtain water at the dams – something without precedent in the history of the village.[42]

Springbokfontein was attacked during the Anglo-Boer War and

taken after 17 hours of fighting.[43] The village received something of a face-lift in 1900 when 100 trees were planted. Of these only one had died by 1902, when further trees for planting were requested.[44] In 1904 the village was described as practically devoid of life, giving

> ...one the impression of a place that has lost heart and has thrown the sponge up. It is nearly all in ruins, – deserted houses of miners, with their roofs fallen in, great piles of debris from the closed copper mine, all speak for themselves. However, there are two churches, English and Dutch, a comfortable hotel, several good stores, Magistrate's Court and gaol, and about a dozen houses, including the Head Quarters of Namaqualand Division of the C.M.P.[45]

In 1906 Springbokfontein was a village with a population of 67 Whites, consisting of 45 males and 22 females, of whom 47 were adult and 20 children. There were 44 Blacks, consisting of 21 males and 23 females – of whom 22 were adults and 22 were children.[46] It is not clear whether the White population remained static between this date and the next date upon which the population was reported (and therefore, whether only the White population was reported), but in 1907 it was reported that Springbokfontein was a 'little village' consisting of 67 persons.[47] It is possible, if the Civil Commissioner's racial prejudice did not blind him to the existence of the Black members of the community, that the population decreased considerably over this period. If it is taken into account that in 1905 there were 44 registered voters living in the village, while in 1906 there were only 24,[48] then it is not unrealistic to assume that a proportionate decrease in population may have taken place during the course of 1906 – and that the total population of the village was therefore only 67 in 1907. The inhabitants, however few, seem to have been an active collection of people since there existed both a cricket and tennis club.[49]

In 1909 the Springbok Public Library was established.[50] Actually the library had originally been established in 1904,[51] but it was subsequently reported that there were no public libraries in the division,[52] so presumably it must have foundered in the interim. The library, it was reported in January 1912, was shortly to be moved into a large hall which had been hired by the Divisional Council from The Cape Copper Company. A school and boarding school were established at Springbok during 1911, The Cape Copper Company giving a grant of five plots of land for the purpose of building this school and boarding school.[53]

By 1913 Springbok still only boasted one hotel. The charges for boarders at this hotel were £7 per month and 10s per month extra for washing. There were no boarding houses and none of the inhabitants was prepared to take in a boarder. This state of affairs led one civil servant to request an early transfer to another division since he considered that after a year's probation he would be in debt. It was in this official's opinion impossible to feed and clothe himself on his salary of £124 per annum. Clothing cost some 50% to 75% more in Namaqualand than in other parts of the Cape Province through which the Government railway passed. The Civil Commissioner concurred in the views of his subordinate and recommended his early transfer.[54] Notwithstanding, the average inhabitant of Springbok must have been fairly well off. In 1914 the first registration of drivers' certificates took place and there were apparently at that time 13 persons with motor cars in Namaqualand. Ten of these vehicles were in the possession of persons resident in Springbok.[55]

The eventual closing down of the mines brought a loss of business to Springbok, but the village survived as a local centre. In the 1930s Carel Birkby described it as possessing the ugliness which marks small mining towns everywhere: corrugated iron, white-wash and yellow dogs without the spirit to hunt their fleas.[56]

Hondeklip Bay

Change in Namaqualand was foreshadowed by the establishment of a trading station at Hondeklip Bay by a Mr Grace – although this station was destined to remain rather small until the opening up of the copper mines, since the boers of Namaqualand were apparently quite unaccustomed to such 'luxuries' as tea and sugar.[1] However, the commencement of mining by Phillips & King at Springbokfontein in 1852, and their choice of Hondeklip Bay as the port of entrepôt, gave a fillip to the development of the settlement. Its choice was dependent not so much upon its advantages, as upon the lack of any other suitable indent upon the coast, the inner anchorage being extremely limited, while its outer anchorage was an open roadstead with indifferent holding ground. Both the inner and outer anchorage were exposed to the heavy westerly winds which blew on the coast. However, in ordinary weather the shortness of the bar, the moderate distance of the outer anchorage and the suitability of the beach for hauling up boats beyond the reach of even the heaviest weather were points in its favour.[2] In any event, whether through the pressure of vested interests or through inertia, Hondeklip Bay was for some years the most important port serving Namaqualand.

The growth of the settlement was fairly rapid as can be judged from the fact that within three years of the shipment of the first copper ore, the number of trading establishments had grown to four – and these concerns were apparently doing considerable business.[3] Its prospect to the eye was not very pleasing, as may be inferred from a description of Hondeklip Bay by John Blades Currey in 1855:

> Of all the dismal places that I have seen Hondeklip Bay as it was in 1855 is the worst, consisting as it did of black wooden buildings standing irregularly in a desert of white sand, the blinding glare from which was insufferable. There was no vegetation, there was no water save such as was brought over sea from Cape Town and as vessels arrived irregularly the supply often ran short. In any case it had to be carefully husbanded and was barely drinkable even after being boiled and filtered. For the prevention of drunkenness there was no Inn, Public-house or Canteen, and the smallest thing in the way of alcoholic refreshment that could be bought was a sixteen gallon cask of Cape brandy, and as 'Man being reasonable must get drunk' the wagon drivers who brought the copper ore down and even some white men used to club together to buy one which they would roll out along the beach and then like the Walrus and the Carpenter sitting down on a rock conveniently low but without any oysters, they would drink it out in a few days, getting some bread and meat from one of the general stores and making things hum in the Township. Authority was represented by a Mr Pillans, an excellent officer and fortunately of Herculean strength who was Magistrate and Collector of Customs,[4] and he kept some degree of order and administered a sound if rude justice for he often had to drag the offender to the lock-up with his own hands and be prosecutor, witness and judge in one person next morning. I remember on one occasion – it was on a Sunday – some excitement was caused by his issuing from his office and sticking up a placard to the effect that the lock-up was full and that any more men arrested would be chained up to the piers of the crazy jetty used for landing and shipping purposes.[5]

Faced with the prospect of having to spend some time in Hondeklip Bay, Currey was so appalled that he considered committing suicide instead.

In its early years, Hondeklip Bay does not appear to have been the most sedate of sea-side resorts. In 1856, for instance, the Civil Commissioner of Namaqualand, Josiah Rivers, urgently recommended the appointment of a Gaoler and Constable at the Bay on account of the amount of drunkenness and rioting.[6] Only a few months later, he again requested the appointment of a Police Magistrate since the Justice of the Peace, one Pillans, was not acting with sufficient force to quell the disturbances created by drunken sojourners and inhabitants.[7]

The road to Port Nolloth was abandoned by 1857 in favour of the Hondeklip Bay road by everyone except for a few Namaqua/Coloured persons who resided at Kookfontein and who continued to use the Port Nolloth route, especially after good rains. The most important reason for the abandonment of the Port Nolloth route was probably that most of the transport riders lived closer to Hondeklip Bay than Port Nolloth. Other factors were that the sandy belt which stretches inland from the coast was wider at Port Nolloth than at Hondeklip Bay, and that the former route was also more badly circumstanced for water than the latter.

By 1857 Hondeklip Bay was the scene of feverish activity. Ships were continually going to and fro and, in a port with such a limited anchorage, this gave rise to continual arguments concerning moorings, chains and anchors.[8] The pier at this stage still consisted of a simple temporary structure. It was later replaced by a permanent wooden one.

To what extent Phillips & King dominated commerce in Namaqualand may be gauged by the fact that, except for two or three trading establishments and a house belonging to The Namaqua Mining Company, all the buildings at Hondeklip Bay had been erected by them. These buildings were, we are told, for the most part substantial wooden stores, offices, stables, dwelling houses, etc. Describing the village, the Geological-Surveyor, Andrew Wyley, commented:

> The wood is covered with tar, which prevents decay, but does not improve its appearance. The ground on which it stands, and for miles around, is loose sand, which is blown about by the wind, and sometimes blocks up the doors like a wreath of snow. The frequent sea fogs are very damp and unpleasant. Water for domestic use, must be brought from Cape Town;[9] that of the Zwartleentjes, three or four miles distant, is hardly drinkable by cattle, so that it would be difficult to find a more disagreeable place.[10]

By 1861, when E. A. Judge arrived in Namaqualand to take up his position as Resident Magistrate and Civil Commissioner, Hondeklip Bay consisted of about 12 wooden houses with a few 'native' huts scattered about. By that stage these native huts were not made of reed mats, as had been the custom, but of old gunny bags or mats which had been handed down. A rather interesting fact noted by Judge was that the inhabitants, from long practice at wading through the deep sand which surrounded the place, had acquired a most peculiar way of walking.[11]

The growing importance of Hondeklip Bay is illustrated by its being made a separate magisterial district on November 26, 1862, with A. R. Orpen as the first Resident Magistrate and Sub-Collector of Customs.[12] In 1865, by which time there were about nine or ten traders at the Bay,[13] a memorial[14] was addressed to the Government from certain miners, agriculturists and others of the Division of Namaqualand. It stated that during the previous ten years, exports from the division had amounted to £800 000, while imports had amounted to £450 000 – the former consisting of copper ore, corn, wool, skins, and ostrich feathers, and the latter of merchandise of every description from Cape Town, on two-thirds of which customs duties had been paid. It was suggested that exports would have been much greater were it not for the poor state of the roads between Springbokfontein and the coast. As evidence of this it was pointed out that there was ore worth more than £500 000 lying at the mines, which was not sufficiently valuable, under existing conditions to pay the cost of freight to the coast. It was also claimed that better roads would have resulted in a greater quantity of wheat being sown. The construction of a line of main road between Springbokfontein and Hondeklip Bay was earnestly requested.[15]

As a result of this petition, a Select Committee of the House of Assembly was appointed to report upon the question of the construction of a line of road from Springbokfontein to Hondeklip Bay, as well as the construction of a line of road from Springbok to Clanwilliam. This Select Committee was at the same time asked to examine a Bill authorising The Cape Copper Mining Company to construct a tramway or railway from Hondeklip Bay to Riethuis – a distance of about 16 miles – which would eliminate the deep sandy belt.

This Committee urged upon the Government the necessity for the construction of a line of road from Springbok to Hondeklip Bay, but considered that the construction of a line of road between Springbok and Clanwilliam was not important enough to warrant the expenditure necessary for its construction. As to The Cape Copper Company's line of rail, they made a number of suggestions to safeguard the interests of the public and added two clauses, the first making provision for the purchase of the line at cost price ten years after the opening of the first portion of the line, and the second making provision for the carriage of the public's goods.[16]

While the Select Committee was still deliberating, however, The Cape Copper Mining Company brought out an engineer from Britain to investigate and report upon the most suitable line of road and railway. This gentleman, a Mr R. T. Hall, found, upon examining the country, that much better facilities were afforded for making a railway or tramway towards the mines from Port Nolloth than from Hondeklip Bay. The superior advantages of Port Nolloth were so manifest that he recommended the Directors to abandon their establishment at Hondeklip Bay and remove to Port Nolloth, carrying a railway of 2 foot 6 inch gauge from Port Nolloth to Muishondfontein – a distance of about 40 miles.[17] In fact, while Hall states that the Directors considered and approved of his plans but their prior commitment to the Government prevented them from putting these into operation,[18] the situation was not so clear cut.

The Select Committee appointed to enquire into the question of Namaqualand roads, in arriving at its conclusions, was influenced by the report of a Mr Patrick Fletcher. This gentleman had been asked by the Inspector of Roads to report upon the merits of lines of road from the 'mining districts' to the two possible ports for the Division – namely Hondeklip Bay and Port Nolloth – to state which would be most beneficial to the Colony and to give a rough estimate of their probable cost of construction.[19]

Fletcher reported in favour of the Hondeklip Bay road despite the cost of construction of a line of road from Springbok (which he considered the centre of the mining districts although in fact it was not) to Riethuis (17½ miles from Hondeklip Bay) being given by him as £20 000, while the cost of a similar road to Oograbis (16 miles from Port Nolloth) was given as only £10 000.[20] It was considered necessary at that time for a light railway or tramway to be constructed from either of these places. The total distance to Hondeklip Bay was given as 75 miles, while to Port Nolloth it was given as 83 miles. We may well wonder why the cost of the shorter route should be so much more expensive. Apparently the reason was that the Hondeklip Bay road was very much more undulating and thus required a great many retaining walls and side cuttings which the Port Nolloth road did not. A further disadvantage of the prospective Hondeklip Bay road was that, because of the retaining walls and side cuttings, it would be far more expensive to maintain than the Port Nolloth one.[21]

The Divisional Council of Namaqualand passed a number of resolutions in 1865, noting amongst other things that from the time of its establishment (1861) the Council had expended the whole of its revenue in vain attempts to keep the road between Springbok and Hondeklip Bay in repair. It noted that a debt of £300 incurred in 1861 in connection with this road had not yet been discharged, although a road rate of 1d in the £ had been levied in every year but one, and that despite all this the road was in a worse condition than ever before. The Divisional Council considered that even were a road to Hondeklip Bay to be constructed by the Government, the expense of keeping it in repair would be wholly beyond their means. The Council thus recorded its objection to the construction of a line of road between Springbok and Hondeklip Bay and protested against being charged with its repair if it were constructed. It seems that the Council had received many verbal representations from the farmers of the Kamiesberg and Hardeveld protesting against the expenditure of the rates paid by them upon the Hondeklip Bay road, which was of no benefit to them since it lay too far to the north. The Council stated that very great dissatisfaction seemed to exist among them, and that their complaints were justified. Thus in future they were determined to expend the road rates upon the construction and maintenance of roads which would be of some benefit to the farming community.[22]

The Cape Copper Mining Company subsequently alleged that these resolutions of the Divisional Council were arrived at '...through the free use of falsehood and misrepresentation', and that the incoming Council would be sure to reverse the resolutions of the outgoing one.[23] Perhaps the Company were not entirely free from misrepresentation themselves in claiming that the Hondeklip Bay route was the one preferred by all the farmers of the division. Judge had some time previously warned that the Company would in the end come to prefer the southern route, as they indeed did, in consideration of the valuable property they possessed on the line of proposed road and in order to monopolise the services of the transport riders.[24]

Fletcher's choice of Hondeklip Bay was in truth not based upon technical or economic considerations, but upon social criteria. In reply to a proposal that he represent Namaqualand in the House of Assembly, he stated, that, in recommending the Hondeklip Bay route above the Port Nolloth one, he was

> ...guided by a principle which hitherto was not considered, that is, the convenience of a class of individuals who have gradually become of importance. I mean the copper-riders, who are also the farmers of the district, and...(who)...are all residing on the Hondeklip Bay side of the mines.[25]

The question of whether or not the farmers were better off for their copper-riding activities was a contentious one. As early as 1861, the Civil Commissioner of Namaqualand, Mr Anthing, had commented:

I apprehend that the magistracy of Namaqualand is not kept for Messrs King & Co. They are prone to adopt an exaggerated opinion as to the great importance of the mines to the community. I hold a very modified view of the great benefit to any but themselves. A certain amount is expended annually for carriage of copper, but this is but diverting the labour and industry of the people from agricultural pursuits to those of mining. The carriers of copper are none the richer for their occupation; on the contrary, almost all the Bastards who have ridden copper are poor, and almost insolvent. Where is the benefit to the community? It is true there is a market for their produce at the mines; but there is also a market at Cape Town, and a much more extensive and certain one, if the shipping place were but easy of access, and a good market established there.[26]

Even Mr Fletcher agreed that the Namaqua/Coloured people had become impoverished as a result of copper-riding, but this he attributed to the excessive brandy drinking which he felt resulted upon carriers joining together when the wagon belonging to one of them was broken. This notwithstanding, he attributed the frequent breakage of wagons to the poor state of the roads, concluding therefore, that if only the roads were improved, then carriage of ores would become a paying proposition. He did not, in any case, consider that the Whites had become impoverished as a result of riding copper ore, quite the contrary. As evidence he cited the fact that from the time of his arrival in Namaqualand, some 13 years before, there had been almost no emigration from the district, and as there were only 134 farms in the division while the census returns had indicated that there were 678 farmers, then were it not for the possibility of earning a living by riding copper ore, an activity which put into circulation about £20 000[27] per annum, Namaqualand would be the most poverty-stricken division in the whole Colony. Certainly Mr J. Rivers, a former Civil Commissioner of Namaqualand, in evidence before the Select Committee on Namaqualand Roads and Tramway in 1865, considered that a great deal of money was put into the hands of farmers by copper-riding, and that, as a result, Crown Lands, if put up for sale, would fetch high prices in Namaqualand.[28] However, Mr E. A. Judge, Civil Commissioner at the time of the controversy who wrote a lengthy report to the Government of the facts as he saw them, considered that the argument concerning brandy drinking was simply '...an expense devised for want of a better argument',[29] and that copper-riding was equally detrimental to the Whites as to the Namaqua/Coloured.[30]

In any case, despite the fact that the farmers were able to ride copper ore, Namaqualand was probably still the poorest division in the Colony. The fact that there were so many 'farmers' and so few farms may be attributed to squatting, and is thus an indication of the extent to which this was taking place. Namaqualand has an appalling record of drought.[31] Drought affected the copper-riders as much as it affected the farmers, and the occupations were thus not complementary but competitive. Evidence given before the Select Committee on Namaqualand Roads and Tramway would lead one to believe that Namaqualand possessed tremendous potential as an agricultural producer. This evidence seems misleading, and one is tempted to think that it might have been deliberately so, since if the Committee had established that the construction of a line of main road would assist none but the mines, they may very well have considered that public funds should not be appropriated for such a purpose.

In this matter one is inclined to side with Judge, who considered that more would be done for the farmers if a large and certain market for their agricultural production could be established at the mines, and this could best be done by making cheaper and not dearer the cost of carriage. Practically the only advantage the farmers of Namaqualand could be said to have had was the certainty of a market at the mines, although even then one must not overestimate the importance of the villages as centres of consumption. A large part of the meat requirements, for example, were met through the use of so-called 'Damara smouse' who traded cattle cheaply in South West Africa.[32]

In the end, the Company opted for the Hondeklip Bay road. They decided not to construct a tramway from Riethuis to the coast but intended shipping also from Port Nolloth if anyone was prepared to ride copper ore there. Construction of the Hondeklip Bay road was thus commenced, the Company undertaking to provide the convicts to be used in construction of the road with transport and accommodation and, in addition, to pay two annual instalments of £800 to the Government to meet the cost of additional establishment necessitated by the works. The Company was, however, released in 1868, following a petition upon the subject,[33] from having to pay the Government the £1 600.[34] By 1869 some £10 000 had been expended upon this road which came to be known as the Messelpad.

A Bill had been passed in 1865 authorizing The Cape Copper

Mining Company Limited to construct a line of rail or tramway from the Bay to Riethuis, a distance of some 16 miles. However, this line was not constructed, mainly as a result of the recommendations of the Company's engineer R. T. Hall, but possibly also because of pressure from the traders of Hondeklip Bay who feared for their livelihood should the terminus be moved to a private farm. Unfortunately for the traders of Hondeklip Bay, their business was soon to dwindle anyway once The Cape Copper Mining Company decided in the late sixties to reorganize their transport system. Whereas at one stage they had maintained a large establishment at Hondeklip Bay, and had paid the transport riders there, they decided instead to grant a contract for the transport of their ores. The transport industry thus became limited to about 30 or 40 men who were paid in O'okiep and who were in addition supplied from the contractor's own store.

By 1870 shopkeeping at Hondeklip Bay had become a thing of the past. A visitor to Namaqualand described the remnants of the settlement:

> Hondeklip is a loose, straggling place on a low sandy beach. It appears from the sea larger than you would expect, and longer than it is. The houses are of one storey; but the huge stacks of copper ore and of fuel quite overtop them, rising to a height of thirty or forty feet, and of such odd shapes that the stranger is rather puzzled to know what they are. Five or six trading stores run parallel to a road which for a little distance is contiguous to the beach, and then curves off, and leaves room for a row of outhouses at one end, between it and the beach, for the use of the Company, and for the shops. The buildings mostly, if not entirely, belong to The Cape Copper Mining Company, and a considerable number are occupied by them as receiving stores. A rude sort of square or market-place is formed in one part, on one side of which is situated the court-house and custom-house, a building of one room, used also as a church. The residence of the Company's Superintendent in the olden times is pleasantly situated on the rising ground a little south of the town, and leading up from the beach, as are also some cottages; the Magistrate, who is also the Collector of Customs, has his residence near the beach at the south end, and the gaol is situated a little back from the shore, in the same direction.[35]

The completion of the first section of The Cape Copper Mining Company's line of rail from Port Nolloth to Muishond, which was opened in 1871, brought about the rapid decline of Hondeklip Bay as a settlement – the Messelpad becoming defunct since it could be used for nothing else but the transport of copper ore. This fact brought Judge some satisfaction because this was exactly as he had warned the Government in his report of 1866.[36] While there were still about 200 inhabitants in 1872,[37] by 1875, at which time there were 12 houses and 11 huts, the population had dwindled to 103.[38]

Hondeklip Bay ceased to be regarded as a separate magisterial district on June 1, 1877, and from this date also ceased to be regarded as a port.[39] At this point there was apparently only one shopkeeper left.[40] When the Civil Commissioner of Namaqualand was requested in 1882 to sanction the construction of a jetty at the Government's expense at Hondeklip Bay, he replied that he did not have the authority to do so, and added '...and...(I)...shall certainly not recommend to the Government that such a jetty should be built'.[41] It survived as a small centre, shipping agricultural produce.

Port Nolloth

Before the commencement of copper mining, Robbe Bay, as Port Nolloth was then known,[1] was important in so far as it provided the Namaqua with a source of income from the sale of seal skins, and as a source of food, since the seal meat was dried and could annually support some 300 persons.[2] With the advent of mining it assumed, for a short time, a greater significance as one of two harbours used for the export of copper ore and, more importantly, for the import of food and capital equipment. Despite its advantages over Hondeklip Bay, mainly in that it possessed an inner anchorage which was safe '...in any weather whatsoever',[3] Hondeklip Bay came to assume the position of port for Namaqualand to the exclusion of Port Nolloth. This was the result of a number of factors; the early closing of the northern 'mines' after the collapse of the copper mining mania of 1854/55;[4] the fact that the Port Nolloth route was badly circumstanced for water;[5] and that the Hondeklip Bay route was closer to the homes of the majority of the transport riders. It must also be borne in mind that there was a fairly large establishment at Hondeklip Bay and that Phillips & King, the major producers of copper ore, owned almost all the farms en route to Hondeklip Bay. These capital investments would obviously not be abandoned lightly. In any event, by 1856 there were only two or three residents at Port Nolloth,[6] and even as late as 1864 it remained a settlement consisting only of some four or five wooden houses.[7]

In 1865 a controversy arose over the choice of the future port of export for Namaqualand, but in the end it was decided to retain Hondeklip Bay as the chief port and construction of a new road was begun. This road was never completed as The Cape Copper Mining Company eventually decided to accept the recommendations of the engineer brought out by them to undertake surveys of the possible roads. They obtained permission in 1869 for the construction of a line of rail from Port Nolloth to Muishondfontein.

Almost immediately, Port Nolloth, which until then had consisted only of the stores of a Mr F. W. Dreyer, a trader, began to grow apace. Even prior to this it had become increasingly important as a port for shipment. In order to obtain the benefit of a customs officer at the port, The Cape Copper Mining Company undertook to pay £200 a year as salary and to provide quarters for such an officer.[8] The population of Port Nolloth soon exceeded that of Hondeklip Bay. In September 1870 a correspondent wrote of the port:

> It is strange how the Government manages its business in some places. For instance, we, with a population double that of Hondeklip Bay, have neither constable nor lock-up, whilst that village has both, and a magistrate to boot. . . . There is no law here. There are about 200 people in Port Nolloth, and I think there should be a lock-up, especially while we have three canteens, and Hondeklip only one, and half or quarter the number of people.[9]

By 1872 the port had grown somewhat, though its appearance left much to be desired as may be gathered from a description given by a visitor:

> The aspect of Port Nolloth, as viewed from the sea, is not inviting. Iron-roofed buildings are seen nestling between mounds of drifting sand; huge piles of what afterwards proves to be copper ore stand prominently forth, as though asserting their importance. . . . A noticeable feature at Port Nolloth, and one shared by most small towns on the sea-board, is the superabundance of flag-staffs. Every house has at least one, and some staffs have no corresponding house. Perhaps a staff is erected as a preliminary step. On the arrival of a vessel, anything that will float is sent aloft, from a red handkerchief to a union-jack. . . . On landing it is observable that the port has its improvement schemes, as well as older places. There is the jetty, which, when completed, will be a great convenience for loading and discharging ships. Down the jetty the miniature railway runs, so that the ore may be brought from Annenous and run alongside boats or small vessels, into which it can be discharged direct, – a great improvement on the existing method of shipping copper. At present, copper ore is brought down by the trucks in bags of about one hundredweight each; these are placed in stacks larger than hay stacks. When ore is to be shipped, one gang of coolies carry (sic) the ore to the beach, while another gang wade (sic) out to the boat, each man carrying a bag. . . . On the right, as we land, is the Customs-house; behind this the

Fig. 17 Port Nolloth from the lighthouse, looking South c1905 (H. R. Moffatt Collection, South African Library, Cape Town)

Fig. 18 Port Nolloth original rail lighthouse tower (H. R. Moffatt Collection, South African Library, Cape Town)

Fig. 19 Port Nolloth from the jetty c1880 (J. F. Goch Album, South African Library, Cape Town)

Fig. 20 Port Nolloth jetty, showing method of loading copper ore (H. R. Moffatt Collection, South African Library, Cape Town)

Fig. 21 Spectakel, showing the mine workings, handjiggers and bagged copper (H. R. Moffatt Collection, South African Library, Cape Town)

Fig. 22 View of the mine workings at Spectakel c1880 (H. R. Moffatt Collection, South African Library, Cape Town)

Fig. 23 Spectakel village c1880 (J. F. Goch Album, South African Library, Cape Town)

Fig. 24 Spectakel pit incline c1880 (J. F. Goch Album, South African Library, Cape Town)

Fig. 25 Nababeep mine shaft c1900 (H. R. Moffatt Collection, South African Library, Cape Town)

stores, etc., belonging to The Cape Copper Mining Company; and at the back of all, the workshops and engine shed connected with the railway. To the left are stores and private dwelling-houses. There are numerous balks and planks lying about; and if you have any pity for your poor feet, walk along the shore in preference to the deep loose sand.[10]

In 1874 Port Nolloth was created a separate magisterial district. By this time a great deal had been done to improve the handling and shipping of ores, a jetty had been built out some 300 feet in length, carried out to a depth of 11 feet at low-water and there was suitable wharfage accommodation and stores for carrying on a large trade. Moorings had been laid down and beacons and a light for the guidance of vessels had been put up.[11] But while there had been considerable improvement of facilities, the lot of its inhabitants was not to be envied. About once a fortnight a little steamer called from Cape Town bringing the necessities of life.[12] Water for the settlement was obtained from a place called Jules Hoogte, about five miles from the port, and was distributed by 'rol-vaatjie'.

The port grew rapidly: thus while there had been only 300 inhabitants in 1872[13] and 448 by 1875,[14] by 1882 there were about 2 000 inhabitants.[15] The appearance of the place had not, however, improved and Simon, later Bishop for the Hottentots, and his fellow travellers received a rude shock when they first saw the 'city' of Port Nolloth from the decks of the *Namaqua*, the Union Company's steamer which plied the Cape Town-Port Nolloth route. An even ruder shock awaited them on approaching the pier. How, they wondered, was one to get up from the boat to the wharf? For those who were still nimble and who had done gymnastics in their youth there was apparently no problem since they merely clambered up an almost perpendicular ladder; for the older, Africa's inventive genius provided a cylindrical basket about five feet high which had an exit in the side and which was lowered to the boat by means of a chain and pulley. This adventurous mode of disembarkation is vividly described by Simon:

Ladies and gentlemen, enter! A whistle set the donkey engine going and you were raised up and swung in the air. Your head was swimming, you screamed. No one paid attention to you. You continued your ascent, and when the time came the derrick transmitted its churning motion to you and deposited you less than delicately upon the landing. *Deo gratius!* We had arrived safe and sound at our mission.[16]

Simon certainly did not hold a very high opinion of this little port:

It was simply a mining camp in the midst of deep quicksands – an agglomeration of shacks, not houses. A few pieces of wood joined together by sheets of galvanized iron made up the walls of the typical house. A roof of the same materials was set on top and the dwelling was finished. It was merely a shelter. Homes, hotels, and even the courthouse were constructed in the same style.[17]

The unemployed at Port Nolloth lived in the most appalling conditions and it was barely noticeable that they were human beings.[18]

In 1886 W. C. Scully arrived at Port Nolloth aboard the *Namaqua* to take up his appointment as Relieving Magistrate and Civil Commissioner of Namaqualand. He too did not consider Port Nolloth the most appealing place:

Port Nolloth is a dreary and God-forgotten looking spot. Nautically, it is an open roadstead, with a narrow channel blasted through a reef of rocks, admitting small vessels in calm weather to a sort of pond. There is a lighthouse, which can only be useful as a signboard telling 'this is Port Nolloth' as the spot where it stands is not more to be avoided than the other wicked looking and storm-smashed rocks around.[19]

In his *Reminiscences* he further described the port:

The settlement consisted of a single row of tin shanties on a sand-hill. Another sand-hill, tired of the monotony of its situation, had begun to travel southward, and was slowly obliterating one end of the town.[20]

But if Port Nolloth was not altogether prepossessing in its appearance, then there were at least many good and kindly inhabitants living there who entertained most hospitably. The village too, boasted its own newspaper, *The Port Nolloth Times*, printed for private circulation.[21] Port Nolloth also boasted a cricket club – the 'Hope Cricket Club'. By 1896 some improvements had taken place. A proper sanitary system was established and the cemetery which had become nearly obliterated by sand had been cleared.[22] All in all, the witnesses of the last century are in agreement concerning the unpleasant sight of Port Nolloth, whether viewed from the sea or the land, and in 1902 we have further testimony to this 'festering eyesore'.[23] By the 1930s Port Nolloth presented an even more dreary and poverty-stricken appearance. Carel Birkby found the poverty indescribable, exemplified to him by the idea of children begging for a drink of fresh water.[24] By this time too, the houses already described in 1927 as rusting away must have presented a dreary appearance. These houses had actually been valued by The American Metals Company's engineer at the ridiculous sum of 1s each, a sum he only agreed to because it was considered that, as they were occupied, some value ought to be given to them.[25]

Spectakel

Phillips & King obtained a lease to work Spectakel in 1853, and in the following year work was begun. A. G. Bain in his report described Spectakel:

This mine, or rather quarry (for it resembles the latter more than the former), has been worked to the depth of about 20 feet, and on descending into, it presents, on the Northern side, exactly the appearance which geologists call an 'anticlinal axis'. It is one mass of green carbonate, and brown oxide of copper, with only some thin strata of gneiss intervening, which latter distinctly show the shape of the anticlinal arch. The bottom of the mine consists of a round mass of gneiss without any appearance of ore; yet the miners told me that they intended to blast through it, as rich beds of ore would be found below: so that there is no telling to what depth they may go. There are large heaps of valuable ore thrown away at the entrance of the mine, which, on account of the heavy land-carriage to Hondeklip Bay, will not pay to ship to England.

The ore sent away generally yields about 45 per cent of copper on an average, and I was assured, on the best authority, that one miner and two assistants will quarry and prepare for shipment a ton per day. This, when worked on a large scale, ought to pay well, being worth nearly £40 per ton.[1]

By 1856 three pits had been sunk. Although two of these proved to be poor,[2] production continued to increase, so much so that by 1861 Spectakel produced a greater tonnage of ore than O'okiep.[3] By 1863 Spectakel was, in fact, the largest village in Namaqualand.[4] The mine soon began to retrogress, however. A school was opened in 1866 but as a result of transfer of workmen to other mines it was compelled to close down in the same year.[5] Work came almost to a halt in 1867, production being only 49 tons, but was resumed in 1868, and by 1869 a mission school had been established. However, as late as 1870, no systematic working had been carried out, though large and 'cavernous' excavations had been made into the side of the hill. E.J.D. described the workings:

An incline has been sunk, and is kept dry, and the ore drawn upon rails by a steam-engine. The vast heaps of refuse are all being carefully picked over for ore, as smelting works are being built, and this refuse will then pay well on account of its fusibility.[6]

The population at this time numbered about 600 souls,[7] but small though the population was, they were not lacking in initiative, and November 11, 1871 saw the issue of the first copy of *The Spectakel Examiner and Times and Namaqualand General Advertizer*. This handwritten newspaper was circulated round the village and contains some interesting information as to conditions at that time.

The editorial complained of the lack of a Justice of the Peace at Spectakel, which made it difficult and expensive to put a stop to disturbances – disturbances which apparently took place daily, and '...certainly to a fearful extent on a Saturday, the day upon which brandy is sold to a greater extent than on other days'. Notice was given of the first free concert and reading to be given in Spectakel, and contained the following warning:

> To stout young gentlemen, married or single. I would offer this advice. 'Do not be seen too often at corners of streets, conversing and flirting with young ladies, even tho' they may be of dark colour.'

The village was apparently also menaced by the large number of dogs roaming around. These constituted an additional threat to ladies in long dresses.[8]

The mine is said to have 'failed' once again in 1872.[9] Some work must have been carried on, however, for by 1875 the population was still some 471 persons. The village at this time consisted of 13 houses and 67 huts and tents.[10] In the report of The Cape Copper Mining Company for 1876 it was noted that operations at Spectakel mine had been conducted only with the greatest difficulty. Nevertheless, the mining captain had as yet not given up all hope of successful exploitation of the mine.[11]

1877 saw the removal of a considerable amount of material and plant, with the idea of abandoning the mine. However, working continued, even though it was unprofitable.[12] By 1884 when the mine began to do well,[13] there were two officers, 20 miners and seven mechanics, as well as 286 labourers employed. A 'Cornish Pump' had also been erected, while a horizontal engine for pumping and crushing was in the course of erection.[14] About a year later it was reported that the postmaster at Spectakel was to have his salary halved from £12 per annum to £6 per annum, since work at the mine had stopped.[15] Six months later it was reported that the low price of copper had caused The Cape Copper Mining Company to reduce their dividends from 20s to 7s 6d, and that the works at Spectakel were 'almost stopped'.[16] Almost exactly two years later the Civil Commissioner reported that working had again been resumed[17] – possibly because of the high price of copper prevailing on the London market as a result of the 'Secretan episode'[18] which was an attempt to increase the price of copper by means of a syndicate. The Cape Copper Company and The Namaqua Copper Company were both members of this syndicate.[19]

In April 1890 it was reported that the people of Kommagas had suffered considerably as a result of the suspension of works at Spectakel. The Company had apparently resumed working, but on a much more limited scale.[20] The mine at Spectakel was valued at £100 in 1891. With the value of buildings and works included, this value was increased to £2 000.[21] The main obstacle to large-scale mining was the cost of transport. It remained a secondary centre, though its condition was continually improving.[22]

In 1899 operations were confined to driving two levels at the depth of 53 fathoms and following ore-ground by stoping between the 36 and 53 fathom levels. The lower grade of ore was passed through the stone-breaker and 21 inch Cornish rolls, from which the slimes went direct to the buddles, and the coarser stuff to the classifiers and Collom jigs. King's magnetic separator was used to extract the magnetite, of which there was about 20%. Some 1 400 tons of ore averaging 31,59% was extracted in 1898. This ore was conveyed by ox-wagon, at about 40s per ton, to Annenous Station, some 60 miles distant, for eventual shipment overseas.[23]

Spectakel was visited twice during the Anglo-Boer War, on February 2 and 4, 1902. The 'enemy' during these visits tore up everything they saw fit – including postal notes – and escaped with £6 10s of public money.[24]

The mine was closed for a short time in 1901, the stopes having become exhausted. Shortly thereafter it was noted that Spectakel consisted of a closed-down mine and a number of stone houses, which were uninhabited and rapidly falling into ruin. There were also two small stores, a post office, four White men and a few Blacks. Water for the village was obtained from the old mine and also from a spring.[25]

In 1911 the Civil Commissioner forwarded an application from a Mr Max Rabie to the Secretary for Lands to open a general store at Spectakel. It was pointed out in this minute that there was one store there at that time and that the mines had not been worked for some time.[26] Although some prospecting work had been done in the period 1908/9,[27] activity on any scale was not undertaken until fairly recently.

Nababeep

Nababeep can have three meanings in Nama depending upon the pronunciation – 'the place where the giraffe drinks', 'the water behind the little hill' or 'where the rock is carried'.[1]

The farm Lelykepad, alias Nababeep, was granted to one Pieter van Zyl in 1850.[2] It was purchased jointly by Phillips & King and John Wild in 1852 for the sum of £1 000.[3] In 1857 Andrew Wyley reported that three openings had been made and a good deal of excellent copper obtained from the western end. The buildings were situated about two and a half miles from the mine. A 'location of natives' was situated between these and the mine. At this 'location' there was a good supply of water. The mine was not, however, in his opinion, a promising one.[4]

In the annual report for 1876 it was reported that a good deal of preparatory work had been done at Nababeep, and as a result, the sinking of a shaft had been delayed. About 50 tons of fair quality ore had been obtained and the mine was regarded as the most promising trial mine belonging to the company.[5] By the time of the presentation of the annual report for the year 1892 a fair amount of work must have been done at Nababeep, though it is likely that it was of rather a spasmodic nature, for Nababeep South had apparently improved considerably in appearance. The superintendent of The Cape Copper Company took such a favourable view of the mine that he commenced the sinking of a new shaft to provide the means for economically attacking the valuable ore ground which he was confident existed there, but the Directors decided that this work should rather be postponed until the ore body had been more fully developed.[6]

The Inspector of Mines reported in 1899 that it was by far the most promising of the trial mines. At this stage adits had been driven into the hill to about 100 fathoms, and a shaft sunk to the 74 fathom level. The 43, 59 and 74 fathom adits had been driven to over 500 fathoms. The principal shaft had been driven to the 59 fathom level and was 14 feet by seven feet. Smelting works, with two of Frasers and Chalmers' blast-furnaces, winding-engine, stone-breakers and air-compressors, were being erected as fast as possible. It was intended to treat not less than 50 000 tons of 6% ore per annum.[7]

By 1902 the mine was no longer considered a trial one. It was the second most important producing mine of The Cape Copper Company. The return from this mine for the year was 11 273 gross tons of 6,52% wet assay. The whole of this quantity was treated at the local smelting works. The estimated reserves were 195 000 tons of 5% net dry assay. It was reported that the new shaft had been deepened to 88 fathoms and it was intended to sink to 90 fathoms.[8] The Cape Copper Company applied for a magazine licence at Nababeep in May 1904.[9] During the year ended April 30, 1904, the returns from this mine were 40 598 tons of 5,85% wet assay. Of this quantity 38 590 tons were treated at the local smelting works and 2 368 tons at the O'okiep smelting works. Notwithstanding the large quantity of ore extracted in the interim, the reserves had increased over those reported in the annual report for 1902 to 210 000 tons 5% net dry assay. At that stage the stopes in the 59 and 74 fathom levels had yielded large quantities of mineral and extensive explorations had been made at the 90 and 100 fathom levels.[10]

It was noted in 1908 that Nababeep was a mining centre with a Black population of at least 2 000 persons. These people were, in the absence of a canteen, resorting to 'drug' taking. The 'drugs' consisted of eau de cologne and 'Hoffman's Druppels'.[11] From various minutes it has been possible to construct the following very brief table of number of persons employed at Nababeep by The Cape Copper Company:[12]

	White	*Black*	*Total*
For the half-year ended June 30, 1908	55	536	594
For the half-year ended December 31, 1908	54	440	494
For the half-year ended December 31, 1909	42	381	423
For the half-year ended June 30, 1910	38	420	458
For the quarter ended March 31, 1912	30	424	454
For the quarter ended June 30, 1912	35	426	461

It is interesting that by 1912 the number of Black employees at Nababeep had overtaken that of O'okiep, though the number of White employees had not. Since the headquarters of the Company was at O'okiep this is not surprising, but it indicates that more work was being done at Nababeep in 1912 than at O'okiep. In 1910 it was recommended that *Part I* of the *Police Offences Act, No. 27 of 1882*, be made applicable to Nababeep[13] which is, in effect, to say that although there was no municipality or even village management board, the village had reached a size where such regulations as this section of the act provided for should be enforced. Since the 'mining centre' was situated on private property the residents had no voice in its control.[14]

Unfortunately, the fact that the village was entirely company controlled has resulted in a complete lack of documentation concerning its history, for, its only history was written up in the documents of The Cape Copper Company, and these documents were all destroyed between the time when The South African Copper Company stopped operations and the time The O'okiep Copper Company took over the Namaqualand mines. The only records which have survived are of a geological nature.

Concordia

The Namaqua Mining Company was formed to exploit the deposits of copper ore discovered on the land of the mission station of Kookfontein or Steinkopf in 1853. Though this company was unable to obtain the support necessary for the establishment of a public company, it was the only company besides Phillips & King to survive the copper mining mania of 1854/55. John Blades Currey, who was appointed its manager in 1854, described the village:

> The buildings occupied three sides of a quadrangle, my house being at one end while the other was left open. On one side were the quarters of the white miners and artizans, and on the other the officers' rooms, stores, blacksmith's shop and kitchen. The Hottentot labourers had their huts at the back on one side and the other coloured workmen lived in the back on the other side. My house contained a large central hall with four good rooms besides kitchen and offices so that taking one room for my private office and one for my bedroom I had always two to spare and they were generally occupied by agreeable guests.[1]

While the buildings were not so extensive as at Springbok, they were more systematically laid out. Water for cattle and mules was obtained from a nearby well, while water for drinking purposes was obtained from Tweefontein.[2] Mining was really a sort of quarrying, and was described by Andrew Wyley in his report on the copper fields of Namaqualand:

> The raising of the ore is effected by picking and blasting, as in ordinary quarrying, – and it is only in a few instances that the services of regular miners are required; but

Fig. 26 Mule whim at new shaft at Nababeep c1905 (H. R. Moffatt Collection, South African Library, Cape Town)

Fig. 27 View of Nababeep smelting works and village c1910 (H. R. Moffatt Collection, South African Library, Cape Town)

Fig. 28 Mine Captain going underground in trial shaft by 'kibble' (H. R. Moffatt Collection, South African Library, Cape Town)

Fig. 29 Concordia c1880 (from the private collection of H. R. Moffatt, Cape Town)

the picking out the ore, above a certain standard, is an operation requiring some care and judgment, as is also the hand-picking of the few washed samples. The last is usually done by coloured boys, who are smart and clever at this kind of work, but require to be watched by some experienced hand. The yellow ore is easily picked, the more earthy green or red ores do not strike the eye so well.[3]

Albert von Schlicht and a certain Henry Home Ley eventually took over the mines at Concordia from The Namaqua Mining Company. In 1869 Ley bought out von Schlicht's share, but excessive transport costs and mismanagement caused the concern to go into liquidation:

...at Concordia the old system was to pay the miners so much per ton for all the ore they could separate from the 'burrs' during their spare time. It was the custom of these miners to hide the ore they obtained by throwing it among the refuse and again finding it, and deriving the bonus. Of course, this could not last.[4]

A group of Glasgow capitalists was, however, induced to purchase the property for the sum of £9 000 in cash and 600 paid-up shares of £10 each, the capital of this new company being £60 000. They immediately began the importation of machinery and the construction of furnaces. Smelting was commenced in March 1872, and by July 1873, regulus and smelted copper to the value of £15 000 had been produced. Employment during this period ranged from between 150 to 500 persons, depending upon circumstances.[5] By 1875 there were ten houses and 219 huts and tents, the population totalling 961 persons.[6]

The census of 1875 had been held on March 7. It seems that shortly after this, conditions changed, for 'H.H.' commented in an article published in August 1875 that the mines at Concordia were still at work '...but with a very small degree of energy'. There were at that stage some 50 tons of pyrites awaiting shipment, but the parties working it had no machinery for dressing the ore. Somewhat sarcastically the writer further commented that the only activity being carried on was the construction of a large new church '...while the existing one was already too large for the congregation using it'.[7]

It is not exactly clear what took place subsequently, but the property seems to have passed into new hands a short while later, for in 1877 the village was described as very small, consisting mainly of the buildings belonging to the 'Copper Mining Company'. The mine was not at work at that stage, the property having been sold to a new company which was due to commence operations in December 1877. The buildings could be listed on the fingers of one hand, being three shops and two houses. There remained then only the church, parsonage and school. Of the recently constructed church *The Traveller* commented that it was highly creditable to the industry of the mission congregation that they had undertaken the construction of this church which was built of stone and was large enough to seat 300 persons.[8] It is assumed that this new company was The Concordia Copper Company which must have commenced operations at some time in the late seventies. They were, however, unable to send any ore away until 1881, when there was a reduction in shipping costs.[9] At some stage in 1882 The Namaqua Copper Company, a sort of outgrowth of The Concordia Copper Company, came into being.[10] In 1886 this became The Namaqua United Company. It was noted in 1886 that the mines at Concordia had greatly improved, enabling the 'Namaqua Mining Company' to increase their yield of ore both as regards quantity and quality.[11] The Namaqua United Company went into liquidation in 1888 when The Namaqua Copper Company was formed with a capital of £200 000.[12] In 1891 it was estimated that the lands upon which the mines were situated were valued at £150. However, if the value of the buildings and works was included, then the value was some £10 000.[13] Little is known of the history of either the company or the village until the Twentieth Century. It is known that Concordia surrendered without the firing of a shot during the Anglo-Boer War, thus allo wing the dynamite stored there for the use of the mines to fall into Boer hands, a fact much deplored by the defenders of O'okiep.[14]

From the time of its inception, The Namaqua Mining Company and its successors had experienced great difficulty in getting their ores to the coast for shipment. These difficulties were not brought to an end with the construction of The Cape Copper Mining Company's railway. In order to understand the situation it is necessary to go into the history of the construction of The Cape Copper Mining Company's railway on which construction began in 1869.

The provisions of *The Port Nolloth Tramway or Railway and Jetty Act of 1869*, were virtually the same as those which had been defined in *The Namaqualand Tramway or Railway Act of 1865.* It is clear from the preamble to the Act that in being granted permission for the construction of the railway The Cape Copper Mining Company was not to be in the position of an ordinary commercial undertaking. In the operation of its railway The Cape Copper Mining Company was to assist in the development and opening up of the country. Once the line was open to traffic a tariff was to be framed which, after ratification by the Governor, would be binding upon The Cape

Copper Mining Company who would thereafter be in the position of an ordinary public carrier.

Construction of the line was commenced on September 4, 1869, and the last rail of the first section was laid on December 23, 1870. This first section was 46 miles long and terminated at Muishondfontein, and not at Nonams as was stipulated in the Act. The gauge employed was the narrow 2 foot 6 inch one recommended by Hall. The rails used were very light, being about 18 lb per yard. These were securely bolted to longitudinal sleepers, 7 inches by 3 inches, and fixed laterally by iron tie rods fastened underneath the sleepers in order to allow free passage of the animals working on the line.[15] Two small engines were at first employed on the lower portions of the line (i.e. as far as the 22 and 35 mile stations). This was quite illegal since the governing Act did not provide for steam-power. Mules were used on the rest of the line. However, the two small engines employed – the *John King* and the *Miner*[16] – proved to be subject to many breakdowns and were also more expensive than mule traction. They were scrapped in 1876, when mule transport was reinstated along the entire length of the line.[17] The opening up of this first section of the line was so successful that application was made to the Government to authorize an extension, permission for which was conferred by *The Port Nolloth Tramway or Railway Extension Act of 1871.*

This Act, as can be surmised from the title, merely provided for an extension of the line by some 12 miles and thus embodied the same provisions as the original Act. Though this extension was only about 12 miles long, from Muishondfontein to a place near the mission station of Kookfontein or Steinkopf, it took until 1873 to complete, because of the enormous engineering difficulties. The course was extremely winding, having one curve of 130 feet, on which there was a gradient of 1 in 19,[18] known as Nixon's cutting. It was then decided to make an application to extend the line to O'okiep. Permission for this was obtained in 1873.[19]

This Act did not embody the same provisions as the previous two in connection with the transport of the public's goods, though the right of purchase established in the previous two Acts was included. The omission of this provision was at the specific request of The Cape Copper Mining Company who, in fact, were not prepared to construct the line if such a provision were inserted into the Act.[20] They had, in any case, been far from willing to accept such a provision in the previous Acts. The Cape Copper Mining Company's objections to the insertion of such a provision were that a more expensive line would be required and that, having carried the public over the worst part of the road, they should not be compelled to carry their goods any further, as this would interfere with the objects of The Cape Copper Mining Company. In accepting the arguments of The Cape Copper Mining Company the Select Committee was, no doubt, influenced by the fact that since the proposed line did not traverse any Crown land there was no *quid pro quo* for compelling The Cape Copper Mining Company to do something to which they were so violently opposed. Moreover the right of purchase of the line provided some safeguard for the public.

The whole distance of the line – 93 miles – was opened on January 1, 1876. The cost of construction was for many years shown in the balance sheets of The Cape Copper Mining Company as £169 218 16s 7d, including the cost of construction of the jetty at Port Nolloth, an average of less than £2 000 per mile.[21] From the beginning there were complaints of excessive charges made by The Cape Copper Mining Company for, although a tariff was submitted by them to the Government in February 1871, this tariff was in its nature so excessive that it was never ratified.[22] This left The Cape Copper Company free to do what it wished, transporting its own goods first[23] and levying discriminatory charges in favour of The Namaqua Copper Company so that they would not object too vociferously. Although the Colonial Government did not have the power to compel The Cape Copper Mining Company to reduce the tariff, they did hold the option of purchasing the line at its cost price ten years after the opening of the first portion of the line. The first portion had been opened to Abberlaack, (22½ miles) on June 30, 1870.

As a result of the excessive charges levied by The Cape Copper Mining Company on their line, a petition was forwarded to the Government in 1880 requesting that the right of pre-emption provided for in the Acts be taken up by the Government. As a result, a Select Committee was appointed to consider whether the Government should exercise its right of purchase. Notwithstanding evidence that the cost of transport, as apart from its availability, had not decreased as a result of the construction of the railway[24] – allegations which The Cape Copper Mining Company rejected,[25] despite the evidence of the former traffic manager that the line was making a profit of 100% and that rates could thus be reduced from 1s 1d per ton mile to 9d per ton mile and still leave The Cape Copper Mining Company a reasonable rate of profit,[26] and the evidence of the manager of King & Sons (the Cape agent of The Cape Copper Mining Company) that the prayer of the petitioners was reasonable and should be acceded to, as the purchase of the railway by the Government and decreased rates which were likely to follow would develop the resources of the country.[27]

The Committee reported that they did not think that the time had arrived for the purchase by the Government of the Namaqualand line of rail.[28] The reasons for their decision were probably; firstly, that evidence given before them indicated that The Cape Copper Mining Company was the sole, or almost the sole, user of the line; and secondly that, even if The Cape Copper Mining Company was making a large profit, they had constructed the line at considerable risk to themselves, and so were entitled to make monopoly profits. What was perhaps not realized was that by not taking up their right of pre-emption the Government had forfeited it, The Cape Copper Company being thereby freed to do what it wished, even to the extent of removing the rails should it so desire.

In running its railway The Cape Copper Company showed the same degree of overlordship they exhibited in connection with the lives of their workers and anyone dependent upon them. Only continual 'nagging' from The Namaqua Copper Company, who had in 1889 constructed a line of rail from their mines at Concordia, a distance of some seven miles, to join The Cape Copper Company's line a mile and a half from O'okiep,[29] resulted in The Cape Copper Company extending differential rates towards them. The Namaqua Copper Company could not, however, complain too much, for The Cape Copper Company could always threaten to throw off their goods when they reached Kookfontein. The Namaqua Copper Company considered nonetheless that even the differential rates charged them were too high. These rates were also considered to be too high by persons not connected with the mining industry at all.[30] The only way to remedy the situation was for the Government or someone else to build a line from Kookfontein to the mining districts.[31] While one section of the line remained free of any Governmental control whatsoever, nothing could be done, however. The managers of The Namaqua Copper Company took up the suggestion and a Bill authorising them to construct a line of rail from Kookfontein to Concordia, parts of which were to run almost alongside The Cape Copper Company's line of rail, was introduced in 1900, and referred to a Select Committee.[32]

The Select Committee approved the Bill and, as a result, *Act No. 7 of 1900* was passed, which authorized The Namaqua Copper Company to construct a line of railway between Kookfontein and Concordia. In terms of this Act, The Namaqua Copper Company was additionally granted running powers over The Cape Copper Company's line. This was understandably an essential feature of the Act, since otherwise The Cape Copper Company could merely have raised their rates on the section from Port Nolloth to Kookfontein as the Government had no control over the tariffs charged. In fact, this line was never constructed, being merely a sort of Damoclean device. A compromise was arrived at whereby The Cape Copper Company reduced the rates to The Namaqua Copper Company. As far as the general public was concerned, the rates remained as high as ever before.[33]

In 1903 Mr Bellechasse Morison was appointed by the Government to enquire into The Cape Copper Company's Railway. He was instructed to ascertain whether, in the event of the line being acquired by the Government, the existing rates could be lowered, while the line still continue to pay interest. He experienced some difficulty in determining a value for the line. This resulted from The Cape Copper Company's lack of records! The Company put a value of some £400 000 upon the line, a sum which Bellechasse Morison accepted as the basis for his calculations although he regarded the value as nearer £310 000. He reported that should the Government take over the line, a considerable reduction in rates could be made, even allowing for all running expenses and interest on the purchase price.[34] He concluded that The Cape Copper Company did not in fact charge themselves for the transport of their ores, but were able to cover working costs upon the tariff levied to others.[35] In the event the Government did not take over the line.

A further investigation into The Cape Copper Company's Railway was instigated in 1905. Messrs Quentrall and Ronaldson were appointed by the Government to enquire into the mineral resources of Namaqualand with a view to the Government's taking over of the Port Nolloth/O'okiep railway. They stated in their review of the state of the industry:

Several mines of high-grade copper have been discovered; some were entirely, and some were for a long time, worked under great difficulties through the high cost of transport. Two of these high-grade mines, O'okiep and Tweefontein are still working, and one low-grade mine, Nababeep, with its 6 per cent ore, is also working, and on a much larger scale than the other two. Each of these mines is being profitably worked. High-grade ore is sent away for treatment in England and the low-grade ore is smelted locally, at O'okiep and Nababeep, and in the case of Tweefontein is either concentrated for shipment or stacked for smelting, in the water-jacket furnaces now under construction. The treatment of comparatively low-grade ores is now possible by means of local smelting, particularly blast-furnace, making use of the sulphur in the ore as a natural fuel.

This treatment of low-grade ores has only become practicable through lower railway rates and the consequent possibility of local smelting, and it is not open to question that the former factor must influence most favourably.

The enquiry narrows itself down to three questions, viz.:– The life of the present mines, the probability of opening out other mines, and the influence of lower rates for railway transport and loading and unloading charges at the port.[36]

They believed that the Nababeep mine of The Cape Copper Company, and the Tweefontein mine of The Namaqua Copper Company, both had long leases of life. They further believed that other deposits would be discovered, and they concluded that prospecting should be encouraged. Quentrall and Ronaldson considered that the acquisition by the Government of The Cape Copper Company's railway was justified and, that after reasonable reductions had been made in the rates, the railway could still be run profitably.[37] A Bill was introduced in 1906 for the acquisition of the railway.[38] This was read for the first time at the very end of the Parliamentary session. However, because of disagreement over the purchase price (not to exceed £320 000) and lack of details and facts which the Government was able to place before the Legislature,[39] debate was adjourned and does not appear to have been re-opened. Thus The Cape Copper Company remained in possession of the railway.

The Namaqua Copper Company was reported to have employed a total of 669 persons during the half-year ended June 30, 1908.[40] This figure was made up as follows:

	Whites	*Blacks*
Underground (miners)	23	249
Surface (mine labourers)	11	297
Office staff	7	1
Artisans	16	44
General (surface)	1	20
	58	611

Figures for the following four years do not appear to vary all that much, though a slight decline is indicated. In the quarter ended June 30, 1912, for example, a total of 562 persons was employed, consisting of 52 Whites, 463 Black men and 47 Black women.[41]

Continual improvements were made for the treatment of poorer grades of ore. In 1905 the Company was reported to be in the process of erecting machinery for smelting purposes.[42] Shortly thereafter an Elmore concentration plant was installed and it was reported that dumps of old tailings, poor oxidized ores, and material generally too poor for smelting or unsuitable for the Elmore plant was being treated by leaching.[43] Operations were forced to a halt at the close of the First World War as a result of the South African Government's decision to stop all exports of copper ore to Britain, so that the cargo-carrying capacity of ships could be employed for the conveyance to Britain of foodstuffs and articles of greater importance than copper. Exploratory work was, however, continued in so far as the resources of the company permitted.[44] Operations were subsequently renewed though smelting operations were finally suspended in July 1930. Production of concentrates by the flotation process was continued until June 17, 1931, when all operations ceased.[45] A short while thereafter Carel Birkby found Concordia

> ...a place of slumbering silence, peopled only by one or two workmen, who, like Irish keeners at a wake, watch the corpse of the mine they once saw alive. An old shopkeeper sits behind his counter, mourning lost trade. Uncurtained windows, like blind eyes, shine dully in uninhabited houses.[46]

The shareholders of The Namaqua Copper Company had nevertheless done fairly well, since the company paid over 400% in dividends from 1888 to 1928.[47]

O'okiep

O'okiep is said to have one of two meanings in Nama depending on the pronunciation: 'the place of the big tree' or 'the little fountain'.[1]

When O'okiep was surveyed in March 1856, it consisted of a small shaft about three yards deep – a shaft displaying a splendid show of ore. By late 1856 working had already been extended to about 40

Fig. 30 The Namaqua Copper Company's smelting works at Concordia (from the private collection of H. R. Moffatt, Cape Town)

Fig. 31 O'okiep, the sorting floors showing the buddle ponds c1890 (H. R. Moffatt Collection, South African Library, Cape Town)

Fig. 32 The O'okiep sorting floors, showing hand jiggers and buddle ponds c1890 (H. R. Moffatt Collection, South African Library, Cape Town)

Fig. 33 Miners preparing to go underground at O'okiep c1890 (H. R. Moffatt Collection, South African Library, Cape Town)

Fig. 34 O'okiep, loading bagged copper ore which had been hand-sorted (H. R. Moffatt Collection, South African Library, Cape Town)

Fig. 35 O'okiep, mined rock being taken for breaking and sorting by hand (H. R. Moffatt Collection, South African Library, Cape Town)

Fig. 36 O'okiep, Black women sorting out copper ore for bagging (H. R. Moffatt Collection, South African Library, Cape Town)

Fig. 37 Mule-drawn train on the way to Port Nolloth c1885 (H. R. Moffatt Collection, South African Library, Cape Town)

feet. O'okiep became in the sixties the most important mine of The Cape Copper Mining Company, and by 1870, when 'J.S.H.' visited the village, he found a scene of bustling activity, for by this time O'okiep, described only a short while later as the richest copper mine in the world,[2] had become an important centre:

> ...if the natural scenery is dull and uninteresting from its nakedness, the industry is different, and is very striking. After travelling for two days through a country so naked, and barren and destitute that for miles and miles around you, yourself and your outfit are the only living, moving things on which the eye can rest for relief, you come at once, after topping the low hills, on a scene of animated industry which has no equal in South Africa, or, perhaps, on the Continent of Africa at all – the results of which are visible in the acres of pure stone in one immense spread, some ten or twelve feet thick, turned up from the mine, and the large stacks of copper ore, and the great extent of the refuse. There are stores, and offices and stables, and workshops, and large deposits of machinery, and a steam-engine and all its gear in full working, and a church (used also as a school and reading-room), and a contractor's store, and an infirmary for the sick, and residences for the mechanics and miners; and in the rocks around the valley are pretty little cottages for the officers; and around the southern and western slopes are the different locations of natives, dwelling in houses of gunny bags, – Hottentots, Fingoes, Mantatees, – each in his own location, and two tribes of Damaras, equally distinct; and at the north a separate location of those fragments of humanity that, cast loose from the main body, pass over the boundary line, and live a sensuous life of illegitimacy. All these, between 800 and 900 souls, and some at Springbok and at greater distances, find direct support from the O'okiep Mines.[3]

By this time the mine was some 250 to 300 feet deep. The classification was described by 'J.S.H.':

> Officers of superior and inferior grades; clerks, miners, and mine mechanics; stokers and a lower grade of mechanics, and labourers of European race and Native labourers: the two latter pass occasionally over the boundary in life's struggle, the one making slight efforts to struggle upward, and the other making rapid strides downward.[4]

Labour was, at this time, organised in one of two ways, both by piece work and known as 'tut-work' and 'tribute'. Tut-work consisted of sinking shafts, galleries and such, while tribute work was concerned with raising of the ore to the surface. In both instances the miner used Black labour to assist him. Blasting was also done by Black labour. In fact, almost the entire process of concentration of ore was carried out by Black labour under White supervision. White miners brought out from Britain earned from £10 to £12 per month, mine mechanics were paid from £8 to £12 per month, mechanics hired within the Colony and who had no special qualifications were paid less. Both the miners and mechanics were provided with furnished lodgings.

Other employees fell into the following broad categories:

7s and upward per day 11 employees

4s and upward per day 25 employees, most of them White

1s 6d and upward per day 135 employees, mostly men who were unskilled

4d and upward per day 122 employees, mostly women and children[5]

'J.S.H.' considered that the wage gap though wide was not too wide when one took into consideration the gap between '...the skilled labour of civilization and the unskilled labour of barbarism', and advanced arguments which have often been put forward since then to explain the wide gap in wages between Black and White:

> The Coloured races are, the majority of them, when they come first to work at the mines, from tribes unacquainted with civilization, they have never seen work done, are entirely ignorant of the use or the names of the tools, and are unacquainted with the language; and all these preliminary difficulties have to be got over before they can be taught.[6]

Workmen apparently came from all parts of South Africa:

> ...no better proof of a desire for industry can possibly be given than that of the great distances the various tribes come to look for employment. There is certainly nothing very captivating at the mines either in the labour or in the rate of wages, which, in proportion to the price of provisions, is not too high.[7]

It is clear however that some difficulty was experienced in obtaining adequate supplies of Black labour. The evidence exists in a letter to the Colonial Secretary from the Superintendent of The Cape Copper Mining Company in which he offered employment to 40 or 50 of the poor of Cape Town at wages ranging from 1s 6d to 4s per day, depending upon efficiency. Underground experienced miners were also sought at rates of up to £8 per month, and these labour requirements were exclusive of men needed for the construction of the tramway.[8]

In 1872, another visitor to Namaqualand, probably E. J. Dunn, described O'okiep in the following terms:

> ...(O'okiep) is ninety miles from the sea, and consists of a group of stone buildings, with iron roofs, situate (sic) on the north side of the mine with a few detached residences built close against the range running along the north side of the village. As this mine and Spectakel are the only two in the Colony, it deserves a somewhat detailed examination. Perhaps the first objects that attract notice are the huge heaps of rock, &c., that are lying about the mouth of the shaft. They have all a certain greenish colour, and are formed of various qualities of stuff, from the large heaps of mixed rock and ore to the heaps of refuse rock from which the ore has been separated, and stacked also in heaps for bagging. The processes through which the ore passes before

being bagged are interesting. As the rock is broken out, it is raised to the surface, and thrown into heaps. These heaps are operated on by 'cobbers' who break each lump into small pieces, separating the solid ore, the barren rock, and the rock with the ore through it. These latter pieces are put through the stone-breaker, and then through rollers. It is then put into the 'strakes'. These strakes are box sieves working in water, with a jerking motion. The effect of the concussions is to separate the heavier from the lighter particles; at the same time, all the very fine material passes through the perforation. This, as it collects in the strakes, is taken out and put through the 'buddle' – a circular, inclined table, with the centre as the lowest point, around which brushes sweep the fine material; and water being led in from the outer rim, all the material travels towards the central outlet of the table, but the lighter particles travel more quickly than the ore. The brushes also tend to check the progress of the latter, as they sweep round, and also to separate the heavy from the light particles; the result being that all the particles of rock are washed through the centre of the table, and the ore remains on the high rim of the buddle. This is also taken out, and bagged for shipment. The various operations here described are performed by natives, such as Damaras, Zulus, Hottentots, Bushmen, &c. There is a great deal of 'picking' necessary to separate the various classes of ores, and for this work they are peculiarly fitted, as their keenness of vision enables them to sort with great accuracy...

The process at present in operation for reducing the ore is by German blast furnaces. A small engine drives the blast, and the ore, fuel, lime, &c., used as flux, are fed in from a stage near the top of the furnace. One furnace will produce about one ton of copper per day. The principal ores used are silicates and mixed ore containing magnetic iron, from Koperberg, &c., and most of it is reduced to regulus. The fire, after being once lit, is not allowed to expire until the furnace requires repair. At night it is a curious sight to watch the great flames dancing, and throwing a lurid glare for a considerable distance around. The slag comes flowing slowly out on to the hearth in front of the furnace and falls as a sluggish stream of molten rock into crucible-shaped receptacles. These, when full, run along rails, and the slag is tipped out red-hot. As these masses cool they become dark in colour, vitreous and brittle. When the furnace is ready for tapping, a steel rod is driven by means of a heavy hammer through the plug of clay left in the side and at the bottom of the furnace. On being withdrawn a fiery stream rushes out of liquid copper, likely, perhaps, to be formed into pennies, sham jewellery, or saucepans – all useful articles in their way.

Rows of holes have been previously dug in the sand, and the stream of molten metal fills one after another. When the slag begins to run, the opening is stopped, and a fresh charge put into the furnace.

If coal and transport were more reasonable, there is practically no limit to the amount of ore available for smelting; but as fuel costs £9 per ton, and it takes two tons for one of metal, nothing but rich ores can at present be profitably employed.[9]

Apart from the measures introduced for improved concentration of the ores, steps were also being taken to improve the means of transport.

By 1873 O'okiep had a population of about 1 500 persons. The mine employed 872 of whom 223 worked underground and 546 on the surface. There were 103 smelters, artisans, stablemen, cart drivers, etc., and 25 officers and sub-officers.[10] Women and children were employed to sort the ore by hand.[11] The mine had by this time reached a depth of 420 feet, and experienced miners took 20 minutes in climbing the ladders from the bottom to the summit level.[12] The ores averaging 30%-60% were set aside for the market, fine seconds averaging 17% were improved by crushing and water-dressing to 35%, while coarse seconds averaging 14% were raised to 28%-30%. Lower grades were put into reserve, while ores of 9%-10% were sent to the smelting furnace to be converted into regulus of 50%-60%.[13] By 1875 there was a population of 1 752 and there were 73 houses and 367 huts and tents.[14] In 1877 a traveller through Namaqualand found O'okiep a scene of some industry:

O'okiep, the copper wonder, lies in a valley, and has only been worked about fifteen years, with its huge water pumping engine, winding engine, and all the numerous engines and machinery required for crushing and washing the ore after it is raised from the mine. There is a perpetual clatter which, to a stranger is very fidgeting, but which is not noticed by those resident, unless there is a stoppage, when everyone looks up to see what is the matter. The people are called to work, etc., by a huge steam whistle, which can be heard for many a mile when wind and weather are favourable. Almost every nation finds its representatives there, English, French, German, Italian, Portuguese, the Colonial Dutch, and 'Africanders', and as for the numerous Native races, I would scarcely like to say what African race was not there. Here you see men from the far interior, West and East Coast of Africa, Lascars, Indians, Kafirs, Fingoes, Hottentots, Bushmen, and the various Damara nations, and all the wonderful crosses produced by marriage amongst such a mixed population.[15]

By 1882 the population of O'okiep was estimated at 2 000. It was a decidedly unhealthy place to live, the setting up of the smelters having caused the air to become unhealthy and even the water to become contaminated. As a result it was not uncommon to have two to three burials a week.[16] There were eight stores which could supply any need and trade flourished since the Company pay-roll was high. The houses were apparently of substantial construction, the roofs being made of galvanised iron while the walls were made of brick or stone. There was an English Church, two schools, a Wesleyan Church and a hospital. Mail came and went twice a week and messages could be transmitted by telephone and telegraph.[17]

An amusing account of a journey on The Cape Copper Mining Company's railway is given by Bishop Simon, who was for many years a missionary in Namaqualand, in his autobiography. Arriving at Port Nolloth from France in 1882, he says:

There was a thick fog and we could hardly see thirty feet ahead. The thermometer read four degrees above zero (36°F), and we were lightly clothed. Would anyone in

France have thought it possible to be cold in Africa! We walked back and forth, we blew into our hands, and looked impatiently into the distance. We were hoping to see the train so we could jump into a compartment and at least have shelter. But nothing came into sight except some mules with harnesses on their backs. We wondered what these beasts could be doing in the African sands.

I cannot describe our amazement when we saw that the mules were firmly harnessed to a few little carriages. Yes, this was the train! These rolling boxes were our dining and sleeping cars, these mules were our engines. Each passenger carriage had three mules, and the freight cars, which were coupled in groups of three, were pulled by six mules harnessed in single file and trotting between the rails. The whole train consisted of about sixty mules and thirty cars.

A whistle announced the departure. Passengers for O'okiep, all aboard!...

The train began to move. I need not mention its speed since you already know the power of our locomotive. Each unit was entrusted to two conductors. One of them, armed with a strong whip, took charge of speeding the progress of the mules should they imprudently choose to slow down their gait. The other conductor had his hand on the brake to control the speed of the vehicle. This latter function was quite essential since the tracks tended to follow the topography of the land. When we went downhill, unless the brakes were applied the car would take on more and more speed until it was practically at the mules' heels. This would have been disastrous both for the passengers and the poor animals.[18]

Commenting upon the section of the line from Annenous to Klipfontein summit, a distance of seven and half miles with a rise of 1 330 feet, he says:

The construction of the railroad on this mountainside is a masterpiece of engineering. The grade was calculated with a view to the locomotives that would some day replace the mules. The engineer who solved the problem certainly gave proof of his immense knowledge. The ascent lasted about two hours, and at two points bridges had been thrown over ravines. These bridges were about sixty-five feet high.

As we approached the summit of the mountain we were reminded of the gorges of Switzerland or the Tyrol. There were drops of over 2 000 feet. The road had been hewn out of the rock and there was just room enough for one man between the 'Special' and the rocks. When we looked over the precipices we felt dizzy. The view was grand, but it was hard to enjoy it because we were terrified when we looked into the abyss beneath our feet. We were afraid in spite of ourselves. What if the road should cave in! What if the 'Special' should be derailed! What if the mules should lose their footing![19]

Mules were used until 1886 when the Company re-introduced, again illegally, steam transport on the lower section of the line. In the first instance this affected the section from Port Nolloth to Abberlaack; its use was subsequently extended to the Annenous Mountains on June 1, 1887.[20] The first engines employed were fitted with condensers and tenders in an attempt to overcome the shortage of water. The condensing apparatus consisted of a large number of coils forming an atmospheric radiator over the top of the engine for its whole length. However, the arrangement did not prove satisfactory due to the high ambient temperatures.[21] The condensers and tenders were then dispensed with and the engines transferred to shunting service between the O'okiep and Nababeep mines.[22] In 1890 the first 'mountain' type engines were introduced. These were rather powerful little engines, constructed by Messrs J. Kitson & Co., of Leeds. By March 15, 1893, the whole distance to O'okiep, a distance of 91½ miles (the line having been shortened from the time of its construction), was converted to steam.[23] Mules were, however, retained for passenger traffic until 1896.[24]

Production in 1884 was about 15 000 tons of 30% copper. There were 16 officers and 82 miners as well as 821 labourers employed (including women and children, and the aged and disabled, who were employed in bagging and mending and other light work).[25] Many of these labourers came from other parts of the Colony and Delagoa Bay. They were, in fact, preferred to local labour which was regarded as unreliable. At this stage wages paid were 2s 6d per day for work above ground and 3s 6d for work below ground, plus overtime pay.[26]

To W. C. Scully who arrived in Namaqualand in 1886, O'okiep appeared a hotbed of sensuality:

> I have never been in touch with a community where there was such a constant undercurrent of scandalous innuendo as there was at O'okiep. In certain quarters what I will term moral unconventionality went naked and unashamed. Here and there among the arid hills surrounding the mines small fountains might be found, and at several of these were mat-houses inhabited by the dusky families of men holding more or less prominent positions in the community. This sort of thing was taken as a matter of course, and was not nearly so objectionable as other relationships which unsavoury suggestion indicated. If what was said about many of the inhabitants were only half true, O'okiep must have been, in the matter of morals (or their absence), as sultry as was its climate.[27]

By 1888 the working population of O'okiep was estimated at more than 2 000 persons. The principal buildings were apparently the English Church, the Wesleyan Church, the Hospital Church, and the engine-houses.[28] There was little 'outside' work, as even clothing was imported into the territory. The Civil Commissioner reported in 1891 that there was supposed to be one tailor in O'okiep but, for all practical purposes, there could be said to be no tailors, milliners or dressmakers in the division, since the one at O'okiep occupied part of his time in effecting repairs to damaged garments and the greater portion of his time in dissipation.[29]

Great difficulty was experienced with regard to Black labour, though demand did not always exceed supply – more often than not it did. The balance depended on an external factor – the weather. When it was a good season for crops there was a shortage of labour since the local mission inhabitants were not willing to go out and work. When there was a bad season, the supply of labour far exceeded the demand. In 1891 there was a shortage of labour; The Cape Copper Company employing 786 Blacks while 925 could have been employed so that there was a shortage of 139 Black men.[30]

O'okiep presented a picturesque appearance to a visitor in 1896, with its numerous trees, the planting of which first required the blasting of a hole in the rock by means of dynamite, and its many excellently arranged gardens:

> In the evening the place presents a rather peculiar appearance. O'okiep lies somc, what in a basin, near where the mass of ore-washing takes place. The residential plaase are on one of the hill sides, and on the other slopes are to be found colonies of Damares-who hold themselves quite aloof and distinct from the Hottentots, encamped on another side, and all within easy distance of the mining centre. The characteristics of the Damara as apart from the Hottentot are very marked. The Damara is a steady, hardworking, reticent, thrifty native. Outside his 'werf' one can always find a few goats, and indications of industry abound. The interior of the hut is arranged with considerable care and with an eye to comfort. The Hottentot on the other hand is thriftless, careless, and happy-go-lucky. His hut is invariably open to the four winds of heaven, and he is altogether a most disreputable character with one god – dop. The tum-tum of the Hottentot drum may be heard all through the night, whilst the Damara camp is silent as the grave, after dusk.[31]

O'okiep was besieged during the Anglo-Boer War for about one month, from April 3 until May 3, 1902.[32] However, no damage was done to the village,[33] but a great deal of damage was done to the railway and to the machinery and buildings at Nababeep and Narrap.[34] At this time the village contained four stores, works, etc., three churches and some well-built stone houses with a population numbering about 1 000, of whom 300 were White.[35]

The early 1900s were difficult years for The Cape Copper Company as a result of imprudent investment in Indian mines,[36] and declining grades of ore in Namaqualand. For many years the average copper content of the ore reserves had been in the neighbourhood of 20%,[37] and 1918 proved to be a very bad year for the two Namaqualand copper companies, with both making losses.[38] The reasons for this were;

firstly, the difficulties with supplies, especially coke; secondly, the absence of shipping facilities, thus preventing the output being carried to market; and, thirdly, the prohibition on the export of matte to England. In the opinion of the Government Mining Engineer the fall in prices was only of secondary consideration. The end of 1918 saw The Cape Copper Company struggling and The Namaqua Copper Company shut down as regards all its chief operations.[39] The Government Mining Engineer considered that The Namaqua Copper Company had followed a judicious policy in suspending all their chief operations in May 1918 on the stoppage of shipments of copper to England. Following this stoppage, the Company had been able to dispose of all its metal to Japan at an excellent price. By judiciously conserving its resources while not neglecting prospecting, The Namaqua Copper Company found itself in a comfortable position, both with regard to its financial resources and to its improved ore reserves in 1919. The Cape Copper Company, on the other hand, persisted with operations until the end of April 1919 in spite of the inability to ship their regulus and of increasing difficulty and expense in obtaining supplies of coke and other materials. The Company then stopped all operations by cabled notice, displaying in the words of the Government Mining Engineer: '...a callousness and want of consideration and forethought...(for their employees)...which...(was)...nothing short of culpable.'[40] A letter to the Editor of *The Cape Times* set out the position:

Sir, – Only a small fraction of your readers can picture the extent of the calamity due to the sudden closing down of The Cape Copper Company. Three large villages are affected – O'okiep, which has seven stores; Nababeep, with eight stores; and Port Nolloth, which is larger than either of these. With the exception of the Fish Canning Co., and the Wireless, Lighthouse and the Customs staff at Port Nolloth, every living person except the postmaster depends upon the Company for his daily bread.

On Friday, 23rd May, all day men dismissed at once, weekly men a week's notice, monthly a month, contract men three months.

Daily men means Coloured labour, about 1 000. Paid daily, their wage was daily spent on today's or yesterday's food. Their wage had recently been reduced to 3s. per day, and before the crisis some families were actually starving. Weekly men include a few white men and more St. Helenas,[41] a very worthy class, holding positions of some trust at very low wages. There are very few contract men. Some of the officials and all the remaining staff of white men will be paid one month's wages on June 1, and dismissed to take care of themselves.[42]

The Cape Copper Company did start up again on a small scale in 1920, selling all the accumulated stocks of ore, amounting to 5 842 303 tons at £202 897.[43]

Fig. 38 The Barkly Viaduct on the O'okiep-Port Nolloth railway c1880 (H. R. Moffatt Collection, South African Library, Cape Town)

Fig. 39 Company's 'Special' on the Annenous Mountains c1880 (J. F. Goch Album, South African Library, Cape Town)

Fig. 40 'Condensing type' locomotive introduced in 1886 (from the private collection of H. R. Moffatt, Cape Town)

Fig. 41 *Clara,* one of the 'mountain type' locomotives introduced in 1890 (from the private collection of H. R. Moffatt, Cape Town)

Shareholders in The Cape Copper Company did well out of their investment for, during its lifetime, the Company paid to the holder of an original share (£8 paid-up), £217 16s 3d in dividends.[44] But such was the poverty caused by the closing of its mine, that in 1920, it was found that the local population was becoming more 'nude' and the more modest females were too ashamed to even come into the villages.[45] It was not uncommon for the Black inhabitants of Namaqualand to eat condemned military horses and camels after destruction.[46]

The affairs of The Cape Copper Company were put into the hands of an Official Receiver.[47] For some time the Company's property was under option to the General Mining and Finance Corporation but, when they failed to take this up, an American consortium, consisting of United Verde Extension, The American Metals Co. Ltd, and Newmont Mining Corporation, purchased the property of The Cape Copper Company for the sum of $750 000. They formed a company known as The South African Copper Company Limited,[48] which did work mainly of an exploratory nature.

In the 1930s when Carel Birkby visited Namaqualand he found that there was neither sound nor soul to stir the silence of the broad straggling streets.[49] The railway, however, continued in service and even after The Namaqua Copper Company was compelled to halt all operations in June 1931, the railway continued in use, being in charge of a single individual, a certain Jack Meadows. It was taken over in working order by The O'okiep Copper Company in 1937. After a trial run they found it more economical, and perhaps strategically safer, to send their blister copper to Cape Town by road for shipment to America. The railway ran its last complete run in 1942.[50] It was scrapped and sold in 1944.

NOTES TO CHAPTER 4

1 G.36 – '57, p. 10
2 S.C.2 – '55, p. X
3 A prospectus relative to the formation of a Namaqualand Railway or Tramway Company was issued in September 1854. The project did not, however, receive sufficient support and so nothing came of it
4 G.3 – '54, p. 38
5 S.C.5 – '56, Q.120
6 S.C.8 – '54 and S.C.2 – '55
7 G.8 – '54, p. 39
8 S.C.8 – '54, p. VI

9 Ibid, p. VII
10 S.C.2 – '55, p. V
11 Ibid, p. V
12 Ibid, p. V
13 G.8 – '55, p. 27
14 E. A. Judge Papers, Jagger Library, University of Cape Town, p. 124
15 R. Bright, *Lecture on Namaqualand and its Mines* (Cape Town, Saul Solomon 1855), p. 20
16 G.36 – '57, p. 54
17 G.34 – '56
18 R. Bright, op cit, p. 21
19 G.36 – '57, p. 53
20 *De Mist Memorandum*, op cit, pp. 219-220
21 S.C.2 – '55, p. 17
22 G.36 – '57, p. 53
23 Ibid, p. 54
24 J. B. Currey, op cit, pp. 102-107
25 G. M. Theal, *History of South Africa*, (reprinted Cape Town, C. Struik 1964), vol VII p. 88
26 The Company is hereafter referred to as The Cape Copper Mining Company. In 1888 the name was altered to The Cape Copper Company, Limited. The capital was also altered, each holder of an original £10 share, upon which £8 had been paid up, being issued with fifteen paid-up shares of £2 each
27 *Prospectus of the Cape of Good Hope Copper Mining Company, Limited* (London, Smith 1862)
28 This was made up of £11 286, for the landed estates, £14 000 for the buildings, the movable property at a maximum of £33 000 and for the mineral rights as well as the stocks of inferior ores, £15 000
29 *Prospectus of the Cape of Good Hope Copper Mining Company, Limited*, op cit
30 Usually the pay limit is said to be 20%, but the prospectus mentions 16%

SPRINGBOK

1 G.36 – '57, p. 6
2 G.8 – '54, p. 36
3 G.36 – '57, pp. 6-7
4 1/SBK 5/1/1, C.C. to Col-Sec., 2/11/1855
5 1/SBK 5/1/1, C.C. to Attorney General, 4/3/1856
6 G.36 – '57, p. 52
7 J. B. Currey, op cit, p. 102
8 G.36 – '57, p. 52
9 E. A. Judge, op cit, pp. 76-77 and p. 83
10 A.97 – '61, p. 3, C.C. to Col-Sec., 2/3/1860
11 Ibid, p. 2
12 Ibid, p. 3
13 A.97 – '61, p. 14, C.C. to Col-Sec., 30/4/1861
14 Ibid

15 P. van Heerde en andere, *Springbok,* (Die Poskoets – Reëlingskomitee van Springbok 1952) p. 14
16 E. A. Judge, op cit, p. 113
17 *The Cape Standard,* 10/11/1866
18 *The Cape Argus,* 17/11/1866
19 E. A. Judge, op cit, p. 113
20 *Cape Blue Book* 1867, FF-7
21 *Cape Blue Book* 1867, FF-7
22 J. Noble, *Descriptive Handbook of the Cape Colony, its conditions and resources,* (Cape Town, J. C. Juta 1875), p. 80
23 *Cape Blue Book* 1882, p. 748
24 'From Namaqualand to Piquetberg Road on Foot', *Cape Monthly Magazine,* Oct 1880, p. 211
25 P. van Heerde en andere, op cit, p. 16
26 1/SBK 5/1/8, C.C. to Commissioner of Crown Lands, 9/8/1881
27 1/SBK 5/1/8, C.C. to Under Col-Sec., 11/1/1884
28 1/SBK 5/1/10, C.C. to Under Col-Sec., 17/10/1889
29 Acc 612 (34), Scully to Willis, 14/7/1886
30 Acc 612 (34), Scully to Willis, 11/8/1886, pp. 9-11 and p. 14
31 Ibid, pp. 28-29
32 Ibid, pp. 19-20
33 C.S.C. Criminal Sessions, Jan 1887
34 1/SBK 5/1/9, C.C. to Under Col-Sec., 11/8/1886
35 A municipality was only created in 1933. There had been a village management board in the late 1800s but it had become defunct (See 1/SBK 5/3/11, R.M. to Under Col-Sec., 20/1/1908)
36 1/SBK 5/3/17, R.M. to Director of Prisons, 26/6/1911
37 See for example 1/SBK 5/3/15, C.C. to Actg Under-Sec. for Justice, 27/7/1910
38 See for example 1/SBK 5/3/16, R.M. to Actg Under-Sec. for Justice, 8/11/1910
39 W. C. Scully, *Further Reminiscences of a South African Pioneer,* (London, Unwin Bros 1913), pp. 224-225
40 W. C. Scully, ibid, p. 222-223
41 N.A. 207, 'Reports of Civil Commissioner concerning a certain W.A.N. Musgrave', 4/5/1891
42 1/SBK 5/3/1, C.C. to Under-Sec. for Agriculture, 13/1/1896
43 Acc.1782(2), Mrs J. Henwood's siege diary. Also Acc. 1783, Boer War 1899-1902 – siege of O'okiep defence orders
44 1/SBK 5/3/5, C.C. to Sec. for Public Works, 16/1/1902
45 G. H. Brumell: 'Namaqualand as seen from the saddle,' *The New Era,* 22/6/1904, p. 183
46 1/SBK 5/3/9, R.M. to Under Col-Sec., 1/2/1906
47 1/SBK 5/3/10, C.C. to Under Col-Sec., 9/3/1907
48 1/SBK 5/3/9, R.M. to Under Col-Sec., 1/2/1906
49 1/SBK 5/3/11, R.M. to Under Col-Sec., 17/4/1907
50 1/SBK 5/3/16, C.C. to Actg Under-Sec. for the Interior, 8/11/1910
51 1/SBK 5/3/7, Actg C.C. to Under Col-Sec., 11/11/1904
52 1/SBK 5/3/8, R.M. to Under Col-Sec., 14/7/1905
53 1/SBK 5/3/18, R.M. to Sec. for Justice, 19/1/1912

54 1/SBK 5/3/19, C.C. to Sec. to the Law Dept, 11/2/1913
Springbokfontein had long been considered one of the most expensive places in the Colony (See 1/SBK 5/3/1, R.M. to Sec. to the Law Dept, 26/6/1896)

55 1/SBK 5/4/22, C.C. to James Crozier, 5/1/1914. Forms for making application for drivers' certificates were issued to the following: (1) Sydney F. Phillips, Concordia (2) Joseph Dembitzer, Springbok (3) Servaas van Niekerk, Springbok (4) John Crofts, O'okiep (5) Michael Waistell Cowan, Springbok (6) Father Westeinde, Nababeep (7) L. Edwards, Springbok (8) E. Rampono, Springbok (9) A. Genis, Springbok (10) 'not running at present', Springbok (11) Hofman, Springbok (12) J. Elliott, Springbok and (13) Lieut Vallancey, Springbok

56 C. Birkby, *Thirstland Treks*, (London, Faber and Faber Ltd nd), p. 144

HONDEKLIP BAY

1 A.97 – '61, p. 8, C.C. to Col-Sec., 14/3/1860

2 G.8 – '55, p. 36

3 1/SBK 5/1/1. Report upon a Memorial of John Shepherd, Chairman of Namaqua Mining Co., and others that a Harbour Master be appointed at Port Nolloth, dated Springbokfontein, 16/5/1856

4 Pillans was actually the Justice of the Peace and not the Magistrate

5 J. B. Currey, op cit, pp. 98-99

6 1/SBK 5/1/1, C.C. to Col-Sec., 10/7/1856

7 1/SBK 5/1/1, C.C. to Col-Sec., 19/11/1856

8 1/SBK 5/1/1, C.C. to Col-Sec., 19/11/1856

9 Water in 1859 cost 1s for two gallons. 1/SBK 5/1/1, C.C. to Col-Sec., 6/7/1859

10 G.36 – '57, p. 55

11 E. A. Judge, op cit, p. 73

12 Introduction to *The Archives of the Magistrate of Hondeklip Bay* by A. F. de Villiers

13 S.C.8 – '65, p. 16

14 A similar petition had been addressed to the Government in 1863, but with no result. H.A. 761, no. 10

15 A.7 – '65, pp. 1-2

16 S.C.8 – '65, p. IV

17 Hall was by no means the first person to favour Port Nolloth over Hondeklip Bay as the most suitable port of export for Namaqualand – both Charles Bell and Andrew Wyley had considered Port Nolloth the better choice, while Commander Nolloth himself had pointed out the advantages of Port Nolloth compared to Hondeklip Bay

18 R. T. Hall: 'The Little Railway in Namaqualand', *Cape Monthly Magazine*, April 1871, p. 251

19 E. A. Judge, op cit, pp. 125-126

20 Though at the time, one of Judge's complaints was that Fletcher did not in fact give an estimate of the probable cost of construction of a road to Port Nolloth. C.O.3096, C.C. to Col-Sec., 21/8/1866

21 E. A. Judge, op cit, pp. 128-129

22 Ibid, pp. 132-133

23 C.O.862, no. 164, Cape Copper Mining Co. to Col-Sec., 9/8/1866

24 C.O.3096, C.C. to Col-Sec., 1/9/1866
25 *The Advertizer and Mail*, 7/4/1866
26 A.97 – '61, p. 6, C.C. to Col-Sec., 2/3/1860
27 In 1863 the payment for carriage was broken down as follows:

Mine Proprietors,	carriage paid	£ 977
Contractors,	carriage paid	2 217
Farmers,	carriage paid	10 315
Natives,	carriage paid	7 472
		£20 981

The Advertizer and Mail, 7/4/1866
28 S.C.8 – '65, Q.83
29 E. A. Judge, op cit, p. 135
30 E. A. Judge Papers, op cit, item 19, pp. 16-17
31 Namaqualand suffered droughts in the following years; from 1784 until 1900; 1784, 1794, 1804/5, 1821/22, 1826, 1836, 1857 to 1859, 1861/62, 1865 to 1868, 1874/75, 1881 to 1884, 1893 to 1896 (J. A. Heese, op cit, p. 11)
32 J. A. Heese, op cit, pp. 225-226
33 A.41 – '68
34 Ann. 223 of 1868 (H.A. 77)
35 J.S.H.: 'The Copper Mines of Namaqualand', *Cape Monthly Magazine*, July 1870, pp. 39-40
36 E. A. Judge, op cit, p. 332
37 *The Cape Argus*, 22/7/1873
38 *Cape Blue Book* 1882, p. 748
39 Introduction to *The Archives of Hondeklip Bay*
40 'From Namaqualand to Piquetberg Road on Foot', op cit, p. 212
41 1/SBK 5/1/8, C.C. to A. J. van der Westhuizen, 1/8/1882

PORT NOLLOTH

1 The port was named in honour of Commander Nolloth who surveyed the coast in 1854
2 James Alexander, op cit, vol I p. 112
3 G.8 – '55, p. 37
4 *The Cape of Good Hope Almanac and Annual Register for 1857*, op cit, p. 171
5 G.36 – '57, p. 54
6 1/SBK 5/1/1, C.C. to Col-Sec., 12/3/1856
7 E. A. Judge, op cit, p. 119
8 C.O. 911, Cape Copper Mining Company to Col-Sec., nos 53 and 74, dated 7/3/1869 and 3/4/1869. The salary was fixed at £100 per annum
9 *The Cape Argus*, 24/9/1870
10 E.J.D.: 'The Copper Mines of Namaqualand', *Cape Monthly Magazine*, March 1872, pp. 165-166
11 J. Noble, op cit, p. 87
12 A. Trollope, *South Africa*, (London, Chapman and Hall 1878), vol II pp. 323-324

13 *The Cape Argus*, 22/7/1873
14 *Cape Blue Book* 1882, p. 748
15 J. M. Simon, *Bishop for the Hottentots, African Memoirs, 1882-1909*, (New York, Benziger 1959), p. 11
16 Ibid, p. 8
17 Ibid, p. 9
18 Ibid, p. 10
19 Acc. 612 (34), Scully to Willis, 14/7/1886
20 W. C. Scully, op cit, p. 182
21 *The Cape Argus*, 22/3/1886. A second newspaper subsequently appeared in 1907 – *The North Western Province's Courier* of which a few issues appeared (See 1/SBK 5/3/10, C.C. to Under Col-Sec., 29/1/1907 and 1/SBK 5/3/11, Actg C.C. to Under Col-Sec., 1/10/1907). The last issue appeared on 28/8/1907
22 'From the Sea to the Mines', *The Cape Illustrated Magazine*, September 1896, vol VII no. 1 p. 4
23 'The Relief of O'okiep', *The Royal Engineers Journal*, 2/3/1903, p. 1
24 C. Birkby, op cit, p. 117
25 *The Cape Times*, 15/8/1927

SPECTAKEL

1 G.8 – '54, pp. 35-36
2 G.36 – '57, p. 8
3 See Table A p. 127
4 1/SBK 5/1/2, C.C. to Postmaster-General, 4/6/1863. See also 1/SBK 5/1/7, C.C. to Under-Sec. Crown Lands, 30/7/1880
5 J. A. Heese, op cit, pp. 216-217
6 E.J.D., op cit, p. 170
7 J. Noble, op cit, p. 80
8 *The Spectakel Examiner and Times and Namaqualand General Advertizer*, no. 1, 11/11/1871
9 1/SBK 5/1/7, C.C. to Under-Sec. Crown Lands, 30/7/1880
10 *Cape Blue Book* 1882, p. 748
11 *Cape Copper Mining Company Ltd, Report and Accounts, 1876*, (London, Unwin Bros 1876), p. 4
12 1/SBK 5/1/7, C.C. to Under-Sec. Crown Lands, 30/7/1880
13 1/SBK 5/1/8, C.C. to Col-Sec., 9/6/1884
14 *Cape Blue Book* 1884, p. 431
15 1/SBK 5/1/9, Actg C.C. to Postmaster-Spectakel, 14/7/1885
16 1/SBK 5/1/9, C.C. to Under Col-Sec., 15/1/1886
17 1/SBK 5/1/10, C.C. to Postmaster-General, 16/1/1888
18 On this see: 'Stimulating Thoughts in Lusaka', *Metal Bulletin*, 7/7/1967, no. 5212 p. 21
19 1/SBK 5/1/10, C.C. to Under Col-Sec., 6/5/1889. The Cape Copper Company had to supply 5 000 tons of metal per annum and The Namaqua Copper Company 5 000 or 6 000 tons of copper ore of a certain percentage
20 1/SBK 5/1/10, C.C. to Under Col-Sec., 19/4/1890
21 1/SBK 5/1/11, C.C. to Census Director, 24/11/1891

22 *Cape Copper Company Ltd, Report and Accounts, 1892,* (London, Unwin Bros 1892), p. 5
23 G.80 – '99, p. 15
24 1/SBK 5/3/5, C.C. to Postmaster-General, 19/2/1902
25 *Military Report Cape Colony, prepared for General Staff, War Office, 1908,* vol II p. 63
26 1/SBK 5/3/17, C.C. to Sec. for Lands, 9/9/1911
27 A. Cornelissen, *Namaqualand Copper History,* (privately printed 1965), p. 107. During the half-year ended 30/6/1908, one White and six Black persons were employed at Spectakel mine (See 1/SBK 5/3/13, p. 989)

NABABEEP

1 *O'okiep Copper Co., Ltd, Summary of Operations in Namaqualand Cape Province,* vol I no. 2. According to an entry in SESA, the name Nababeep is derived from two Nama words, 'Naba' meaning an animal's neck or hump, and 'bib' meaning a small spring. (*Standard Enclylopaedia of Southern Africa,* Cape Town, Nassau Ltd 1973), vol 8 p. 21
2 Grant 1850/Clm Q. 8/24 of 17 620 m to Pieter van Zyl
3 T. 250 and T. 261 of 27/8/1852
4 G.36 – '57, p. 9
5 *Cape Copper Mining Company Ltd, Report and Accounts, 1876,* op cit, p. 5
6 *Cape Copper Company Ltd, Report and Accounts, 1892,* op cit, p. 5
7 G.80 – '99, pp. 13-14
8 *Cape Copper Company Ltd, Report and Accounts, 1902,* (London, Unwin Bros 1902), pp. 9-10
9 1/SBK 5/3/6, Actg Relieving M. to Under Col-Sec., 19/5/1904
10 *Cape Copper Company Ltd, Report and Accounts, 1904,* (London, Unwin Bros 1904), pp. 3-4
11 1/SBK 5/3/12, R.M. to Sec. to the Law Dept, 26/8/1908
12 Compiled from minutes in the following volumes: 1/SBK 5/3/13, 5/3/15 and 5/3/18
13 1/SBK 5/3/15, C.C. to Sec. to the Law Dept, 15/3/1910. It was simultaneously recommended that this Act be made applicable to Concordia and O'okiep
14 1/SBK 5/3/16, C.C. to Actg Under-Sec. for the Interior, 14/11/1910

CONCORDIA

1 J. B. Currey, op cit, p. 101
2 G.36 – '57, p. 12
3 Ibid, p. 53
4 E.J.D., op cit, p. 170
5 *The Cape Argus,* 14/8/1873
6 *Cape Blue Book* 1882, p. 748
7 H.H: 'The Cape Revisited', *The Cape Monthly Magazine,* Aug 1875, p. 127
8 'From Namaqualand to Piquetberg Road on Foot', op cit, p. 208
9 P. van Heerde en andere, op cit, p. 16
10 1/SBK 5/1/8, C.C. to Assistant Treasurer, 4/9/1882

11 1/SBK 5/1/9, C.C. to Under Col-Sec., 15/1/1886
12 S.C.7 – '00, pp. 72-73
13 1/SBK 5/1/11, C.C. to Census Director, 24/11/1891
14 'The Relief of O'okiep', op cit, p. 2. See also Acc. 1783
15 R. T. Hall, op cit, p. 253
16 *The Cape Argus*, 22/7/1873
17 'Report of the Traffic Manager', N. E. Moffatt
18 Ibid
19 *Act 24 of 1873*
20 *Cape Parliamentary Debates*, 23/6/1873
21 Although this figure was carried in the balance sheet, the actual cost was apparently closer to £180 000, A.17 – '80, Q.182
22 A.7 – '00, pp. 5-6
23 A.20 – '74, Q.71
24 A.17 – '80, Q.10
25 Ibid, pp. 14-15
26 Ibid, pp. 8-9
27 Ibid, Q.168
28 Ibid, p. III
29 1/SBK 5/1/10, C.C. to Under Col-Sec., 6/5/1889
30 S.C.14 – '99, p. 31
31 Ibid, p. 36
32 S.C. 7 – '00, *Select Committee on the Namaqua Copper Company Railway Bill*
33 *Cape Hansard*, 1906, p. 634 col. 2
34 A.27 – '03, p. 6
35 Ibid, pp. 6-8
36 G.11 – '05, p. 10
37 Ibid, p. 12
38 A.B. 66 – '06
39 P.M.O.215, no. 138, Chief Clerk Prime Minister's Office to Messrs King & Co., 22/8/1906
40 1/SBK 5/3/13, p. 989
41 1/SBK 5/3/18, R.M. to Asst-Registrar of Births and Deaths, 11/7/1912
42 1/SBK 5/3/8, Actg-C.C. to Under-Sec. for Agriculture (undated), probably 11/8/1905 (see p. 236)
43 *Official Yearbook of the Union of South Africa, 1910-1916*, p. 443
44 Ann. 647 – 1920, pp. 7-8
45 Owen Letcher: 'Namaqualand; Cradle of Mineral Development in Southern Africa', *The Mining and Industrial Magazine*, 11/5/1932, p. 188
46 Carel Birkby, op cit, p. 153
47 Owen Letcher, op cit, p. 187

O'OKIEP

1 *O'okiep Copper Co. Ltd, Summary of Operations in Namaqualand Cape Province*, op cit. According to an entry in SESA O'okiep is derived from the Nama word 'u-gieb' which means the big brackish place (*Standard Encyclopaedia of Southern Africa*, op cit) p. 312

2 J. Noble, op cit, p. 81

3 'J.S.H.', op cit, p. 46

4 Ibid, Aug. 1870, p. 91

5 Ibid, pp. 92-93. The Civil Commissioner in 1875 in reference to his inability to collect house-duty in Namaqualand pointed out that the wages, paid daily, for surface labourers was extremely low. What is more, the valuation of the habitations was in many instances from only 3d to 9d. 1/SBK 5/1/6, C.C. to Col-Sec., 26/6/1875

6 Ibid, pp. 93-94

7 Ibid, p. 94

8 C.O.911, no.100, Superintendent, Cape Copper Mining Co., to Col-Sec., 4/6/1869

9 'E.J.D.', op cit, pp. 167-169

10 *The Cape Argus*, 12/8/1873

11 *The Cape Argus*, 5/8/1873

12 *The Cape Argus*, 2/8/1873

13 *The Cape Argus*, 5/8/1873

14 *Cape Blue Book* 1882, p. 748

15 'From Namaqualand to Piquetberg Road on Foot', op cit, p. 210

16 In 1875 there were apparently some 300 deaths in a population not exceeding 1 600 people. The cause of these deaths was a sort of typhoid fever and famine dysentery (See 'H.H.', op cit, p. 126)

17 J. M. Simon, op cit, pp. 18-19

18 Ibid, pp. 12-13

19 Ibid, pp. 15-16

20 'From the Sea to the Mines', op cit, p. 35

21 H. R. Moffatt, *The Railway and Transport in Early Namaqualand*, unpublished paper

22 Verbal communication, H. R. Moffatt

23 'From the Sea to the Mines', op cit, pp. 35-36

24 Passengers were transported free of charge by the Company – not from any philanthropic motives, but because legally they should not have transported them at all. By not charging, and thus not issuing tickets, they were able to indemnify themselves

25 *Cape Blue Book* 1884, p. 431

26 1/SBK 5/1/8, C.C. to Under-Sec. for Native Affairs, 29/12/1884

27 W. C. Scully, op cit, pp. 226-227

28 *General Directory of South Africa, 1888* (Cape Town, Dennis Edwards & Co 1888), pp. 257-258

29 1/SBK 5/1/11, C.C. to Director of the Census, 29/12/1891

30 N.A. 212, C.C. to Under-Sec. Native Affairs, 11/12/1891. See Table D, pp. 134-135

31 'From the Sea to the Mines', op cit, part II p. 38

32 Acc. 1782 (2), Mrs J. Henwood's siege diary. See also Acc. 1783

33 'The Relief of O'okiep', op cit, p. 1

34 *The Cape Copper Company Ltd, Report and Accounts, 1902*, op cit, pp. 7-8

35 Military Report, op cit, p. 74

36 A. Cornelissen, op cit, pp. 81-82

37 O. Letcher: 'Namaqualand Cradle of Mineral Development in Southern Africa', *The Mining and Industrial Magazine*, 11/5/1932, p. 187. In 1902 it was estimated that the visible underground reserves were 9 024 tons of 21%. In 1904 reserves had declined to 7 000 tons at 21%, though it must be borne in mind that a good

deal of ore had been shipped in the interim. (See *Cape Copper Company Ltd, Report and Accounts, 1902*, and *1904*)

38 The Cape Copper Company had made profits of £17 244 in 1915 and of £33 212 in 1916 (see U.G. 37 – '16). Profits in 1917 amounted to £131 248 (see U.G. 40 – '17)

39 U.G. 38 – '19, pp. 113-114

40 U.G. 50 – '20, p. 113

41 Because the local Blacks returned annually to their reserves at ploughing and harvesting times, The Cape Copper Company imported labour from St. Helena (see 1/SBK 5/3/11, C.C. to Sec. Native Affairs Dept, 22/8/1907)

42 *The Cape Times*, 28/5/1919 (Letter from T. G. le Mesurier)

43 U.G. 40 – '21, p. 117

44 'The Story of Copper Mining in Namaqualand', *The Mining and Industrial Magazine*, 18/5/1927, p. 254

45 Ann. 647 – 1920, p. 3

46 Ibid, p. 17

47 'The Story of Copper Mining in Namaqualand', op cit, p. 255

48 Ibid and 'Nababeep and East O'okiep', *Fortune Magazine*, Jan 1947, p. 156

49 C. Birkby, op cit, p. 157

50 A. Cornelissen, op cit, p. 53

Epilogue

The O'okiep Copper Company was incorporated on May 29, 1937, with a capital of £1 600 000, consisting of 3 200 000 shares of 10s each. In the first instance only 968 400 shares were issued and fully paid up. These shares were subscribed for at $ 2,50 (Canadian) per share by The Newmont Mining Corporation, The American Metal Company, Rhodesian Anglo-American (which soon sold its interest), International Minerals and Metals Corporation and certain other Canadian interests. A further 796 800 shares were reserved for the conversion of notes. An additional 1 200 000 shares were subscribed for and were subject to call. Of the total issue, including the convertible notes, The Newmont Mining Corporation held nearly 67%.[1]

Had the total issue been called up (2 960 000 shares) the company would have had a capital of £1 480 000 – a sum which was considered necessary to purchase the property of The South African Copper Company and to commence working. However, since the assets and liabilities of The South African Copper Company were purchased for the sum of £537 870 15s 8d, (U.S. $ 2 667 000) – a price which included a hidden asset in that The O'okiep Copper Company was not required to pay any South African income tax until all capital expenditure, made not only by itself, but also by The South African Copper Company, had been recovered – the company found itself in an overcapitalized position. By redeeming the promissory notes at par, and cancelling the shares held for contingencies, the issued capital was finally limited to 1 021 056 shares – which still remains the capital of the company today.

The assets of The South African Copper Company consisted of mineral holdings of 105 000 acres, and the mineral rights to a further 50 000 acres, as well as various items of plant and equipment, the narrow-gauge railway to Port Nolloth, and the jetty at that port. Ore reserves at the time of take-over were estimated at:

Mine	*Short Tons*	*Grade*
Nababeep	6 000 000	2,52%
East O'okiep	2 675 000	2,33%
Narrap	625 000	2,18%
	10 200 000	2,45%

In August 1939, The O'okiep Copper Company was able to purchase the mineral leases held by The Namaqua Copper Company for the sum of £2 125. They thus came to own not only all the actual mines in Namaqualand, but also the more important prospects in the division.

The company commenced the installation of a new plant at Nababeep and the rehabilitation of the Nababeep South Mine in 1937. A mining, milling and power plant was completed at O'okiep, and the East O'okiep Mine came into production in April 1945. A mining plant was completed at Wheal Julia (which had been one of the properties of The Namaqua Copper Company) and this mine came into production during the latter half of 1951.[2]

Milling operations were commenced by the company early in 1940, and smelting was instituted in August of that year when 473 tons were produced. A contract was entered into with the British Ministry of Supply for the delivery of not more than 12 000 tons of copper per annum. The year ending June 30, 1941 saw a production of about 11 000 tons of blister copper. Production for the year ending in June 1942 was approximately the same.

In 1942 an advance of $1 400 000 was made to the company by the United States Government's Metals Reserves Company in order to increase wartime supplies. Since the Executive Vice-President of the Metals Reserve Company was Mr Henry De Witt Smith, who had launched construction at O'okiep in 1937, he would have been aware of the potential of the mines. This loan was repaid by 1947. Production in 1943 rose to more than 13 000 tons and, as may be seen from Table E (p. 136), increased rapidly with the advent of peace and a higher price for copper.[3]

The company paid its first dividend in 1946 – this was at 10%. Profits had, however, been made from the very first year of production (1941) when sales of copper, silver and gold (Namaqualand copper contains traces of silver and gold), totalled £467 010 15s 11d, while profits amounted to £109 125 17s 4d, this amount being transferred to the earned surplus account. Subsequent to the payment of the first dividend, Newmont Mining Corporation, (which performs certain management functions for The O'okiep Copper Company at a fee of $3 000 per month), offered shares in The O'okiep Copper Company to their shareholders and thus, indirectly to the United States public. The stock issue eliminated a double taxation problem and fixed a market price for shares of The O'okiep Copper Company.

The O'okiep Copper Company continued initially to use the narrow-gauge railway to Port Nolloth, which they attempted to improve. The railway proved too expensive to run and road transport to Port Nolloth from the mines was substituted, but this, too, was soon abandoned. Port Nolloth was abandoned as a shipping port because of inadequate facilities, and possibly because of the unprotected nature of the port during a time when enemy submarine action along our coasts was feared. The railway was scrapped and sold in 1944,[4] its rails now being used to carry overhead power lines.[5] The blister copper[6] produced by The O'okiep Copper Company is presently transported by road to Bitterfontein (the railhead) whence it is carried by rail to Cape Town for shipment overseas where it undergoes the final electrolytic refining process.

Had the problem of transport been solved, there would still have remained a potentially even greater problem – the supply of sufficient water for the concentration processes, for which the company requires some 1 000 000 gallons of water per day. When this company purchased the property of The Namaqua Copper Company in 1939, it was not only to acquire the workable residual ore deposits, but more immediately in order to utilize the water in the shafts. However, these supplies were soon found insufficient to meet requirements, and a pipeline was laid to a large alluvial basin in the Buffel's River, some 15 miles from Nababeep and 35 miles from Carolusberg (the newest of the company's mines). This pipeline was completed in 1947. At present some recycling of water does take place – sewerage effluent, for example, is treated for use in the power-house – but continued drought is causing some concern to the extent that it has been decided to construct a pipeline to the Orange River.

The O'okiep Copper Company has been one of the Republic's most important producers of copper ore. In Namaqualand the company forms a bulwark against retrogression. A large number of Whites (1 036), Coloureds (1 996) and Africans (2 080) are employed by the company. The market these people provide for the produce of local agriculturists is most important. The farmers of Namaqualand are too distant to supply national markets; should the mines fail, they would be severely affected. For the large number of Coloured persons employed, the failure of the mines would be disastrous.

The company has undertaken an extensive amount of development work. A team of some 17 geologists and geophysicists are employed in this connection. During the calendar year 1972, R1 303 485 was expended on geological, geophysical and diamond drilling exploration.

It was contemplated that a like amount would be expended during 1973.

Although no major new finds have been made, tonnage additions to existing ore bodies since 1967 have reversed the downward trend in ore reserves although the grade of reserves has continually declined.[7] At existing production rates the mines have a life of ten years.[8] Continuing geological research might either bring to light new ore bodies or increase the extent of existing ones, or both. The price of copper must also be taken into account: the higher the price the lower the pay limit.[9]

It is pointless to speculate on the probable life of the mines. In 1892, in a strictly confidential minute, the then Civil Commissioner of Namaqualand, W. C. Scully, wrote that he felt it his duty to report that the prospects of the mining industry in Namaqualand were 'very gloomy indeed'. Scully considered that, at existing production rates and treating only payable ore, the mines had a life of only four years.[10] The underground reserves of The Cape Copper Company's main producing mine, O'okiep, were in 1892 estimated at 72 000 tons of 21% ore.[11] A pessimistic prognosis is therefore untenable, though total dependence of a community upon a wasting asset is not a desirable state of affairs. In the past Namaqualand has experienced the poverty and hardship resultant upon closing down of the mines. Let us hope that she will not go through this process again in the near future.

NOTES TO EPILOGUE

1 'O'okiep Starts Production', *The South African Mining and Engineering Journal*, 31/8/1940, p. 788

2 J. M. Macleod and D. de N. Wiid: 'The O'okiep Copper Company in South Africa', *The South African Mining and Engineering Journal*, 20/11/1954, p. 467

3 See Table B, pp. 129-132, for copper prices since 1855

4 J. M. Macleod and D. de N. Wiid, op cit, p. 467

5 *Namaqualand Copper 1852-1952*, (Cape Town, R. Beerman 1952), p. 5

6 For a description of mining, milling and smelting, see ibid, pp. 14-27

7 See Table F, p. 137

8 See Table G, p. 137, which shows mine production for the year ended 31/12/1972

9 On attempts to control the world price of copper see: 'Stimulating Thoughts in Lusaka', op cit, pp. 19-25

10 1/SBK 5/1/12, C.C. to Assistant Commissioner of Crown Lands, 17/4/1892

11 *Cape Copper Company Ltd, Report and Accounts, 1892*, op cit, pp. 4-5

TABLE A

Exports of copper ore by mine of origin

Year	Springbok	O'okiep	Spectakel	Nababeep	Concordia	Total Exports	Value
1852						31	650
1853						199	3 346
1854	Almost all the ore shipped during this period came from					1 084	25 056
1855	Springbokfontein, Spectakel and Concordia mines.					1 864	54 337
1856	1 500		600		500	2 067	77 749
1857	2 100	40	870		1 000	3 438	102 055
1858	1 685	635	1 184		no return	4 289	127 182
1859	1 020	667	1 200		no return	3 803	113 514
1860	1 009	964½	1 345		no return	3 129	91 540
1861	437	1 254	1 320		321	2 197	61 442
1862	no return	1 400	1 200		200	3 396	93 565
1863		2 311	1 283	100	760	3 540	103 214
1864		3 591	1 075	220	882	4 323	122 602
1865		2 730	563	680	750	4 500	118 297
1866		4 236	293	179	700	4 233	88 732
1867		4 677	49	no return	165	5 605	120 521
1868		6 335	no return		137	2 900	60 985
1869		6 085	1 101			5 581	114 031
1870		6 085	1 101			7 300	146 368
1871		6 660	1 395			7 351	160 956
1872		not known	not known			13 240	328 458
1873			825	smelted ore	260	11 570	312 221
1874			not known			13 646	321 434
1875	approx.	12 000	3 000			12 418	248 537
1876	approx.	12 000	3 000			12 869	257 155
1877	approx.	12 000	240			15 244	303 645
1878	approx.	12 000	297			12 641	252 485
1879	approx.	12 000	?			14 178	283 885
1880	the mines yielded 16 256 tons, Spectakel approx. 1 200 tons					15 310	306 790
1881	the mines yielded about 14 000 tons					13 134	261 110
1882		15 744	1 874			19 669	394 032
1883	the mines yielded about 15 000 tons				617	22 705	454 113
1884	the mines yielded about 21 000 tons					20 348	405 415
1885	O'okiep, Spectakel and Springbok 17 000 tons				1 800	20 213	395 675
1886	38	18 752	72		1 800	28 429	559 328
1887	O'okiep, Spectakel and Springbok 27 400 tons				3 500	28 264	577 053
1888	O'okiep, Spectakel and Springbok 29 712 tons				5 000	40 023	356 803
1889	O'okiep, Spectakel and Springbok 25 000 tons				7 000	32 338	696 918
1890	O'okiep, Spectakel and Springbok 25 300 tons				5 000	32 674	694 356
1891	O'okiep and Spectakel 26 286 tons				3 500	23 691	254 184
1892	O'okiep and Spectakel 31 197 tons				1 700	25 459	253 681
1893	O'okiep and Spectakel 29 608 tons				3 500	18 495	202 316
1894		26 969	1 812		5 500	27 077	284 800
1895		28 489	1 578		6 675	23 545	246 597
1896	O'okiep and Spectakel 30 050 tons				7 325	20 843	218 422
1897	O'okiep and Spectakel 30 977 tons				8 000	27 329	300 772
1898	O'okiep and Spectakel 27 722 tons				9 100	24 808	262 830

Year	Springbok	O'okiep	Spectakel	Nababeep	Concordia	Total Exports	Value
1899	O'okiep and Spectakel 24 773 tons				10 075	25 693	446 985
1900	O'okiep and Spectakel 33 657 tons				9 021	30 032	498 552
1901	O'okiep and Spectakel 33 656 tons				11 700	33 755	571 031
1902	O'okiep, Spectakel and Nababeep 18 412 tons				8 984	16 053	273 366
1903	O'okiep, Spectakel and Nababeep 51 555 tons				13 000	37 284	457 205
1904	O'okiep, Spectakel and Nababeep 71 540 tons				12 559	29 931	514 286
1905	O'okiep, Spectakel and Nababeep 82 334 tons				12 520	30 789	573 076
1906	O'okiep, Spectakel and Nababeep 74 416 tons				10 937	23 967	481 649
1907	O'okiep, Spectakel and Nababeep 72 558 tons				6 347	17 810	557 395
1908	O'okiep, Spectakel and Nababeep 75 280 tons				33 428	22 611	418 250
1909	O'okiep, Spectakel and Nababeep 74 340 tons				32 654	18 945	430 892

The sources for the above figures are on the whole *Cape Blue Books* and *Statistical Registers*. They are not, however, either entirely consistent or reliable. Production for Spectakel, for instance, for a number of years is given as approximately 3 000 tons. It is known from the company reports that production in two of those years, 1877 and 1878, was in fact 240 and 297 tons respectively. Nevertheless these are the most reliable figures available, nor is it clear exactly what the figures constituted by way of type of concentration.

Year	Output Exported	Value Exported	Year	Output Exported	Value Exported
1910	—	401 206	1924	3 384	187 745
1911	21 019	503 908	1925	2 995	160 074
1912	16 951	507 836	1926	3 274	165 017
1913	13 095	369 528	1927	2 909	141 779
1914	14 369	372 028	1928	2 802	164 315
1915	13 973	517 208	1929	2 521	171 694
1916	10 599	474 076	1930	1 315	69 211
1917	10 525	550 642	1931	5 735	37 578
1918	1 669	68 622	1932	—	—
1919	276	17 656	1933	108	1 502
1920	7 892	255 157	1934	—	—
1921	113	5 026	1935	—	—
1922	706	38 622	1936	28	362
1923	2 846	159 713	1937	1	54

(Source: *Official Yearbooks* and *Union Statistics for Fifty Years*)

TABLE B

Copper Prices 1855-1972

Year	Average price of best selected copper in London £ s d	Year	Average price of best selected copper in London £ s d
1855	129 0 0	1885	48 16 8
1856	123 0 0	1886	44 10 6
1857	124 0 0	1887	48 4 0
1858	108 0 0	1888	79 11 4
1859	112 7 0	1889	55 3 10
1860	109 13 0	1890	61 11 10
1861	102 12 0	1891	56 11 2
1862	100 12 0	1892	49 18 10
1863	98 17 0	1893	48 3 11
1864	101 8 0	1894	43 12 8
1865	94 7 0	1895	47 1 4
1866	91 14 0	1896	50 13 8
1867	82 8 0	1897	52 5 8
1868	78 15 0	1898	55 9 8
1869	77 10 0	1899	78 2 7
1870	72 13 0	1900	78 8 6
1871	77 10 0	1901	73 7 2
1872	104 5 0	1902	56 13 8
1873	95 18 0	1903	63 0 10
1874	89 12 0	1904	63 0 3
1875	90 0 0	1905	74 11 5
1876	83 0 0	1906	—
1877	75 16 0	1907	—
1878	68 11 0	1908	—
1879	64 5 0	1909	—
1880	69 5 0	1910	—
1881	68 0 0	1911	—
1882	73 0 0	1912	—
1883	69 3 3	1913	—
1884	60 9 6		

Year	*Average price per ton*	
1914	£62,6	
1915	79,6	
1916	125,2	
1917	125,0	
1918	113,5	
1919	86,0	
1920	80,4	
1921	57,6	
1922	61,6	
1923	66,5	
1924	60,0	
1925	64,7	
1926	63,6	
1927	59,5	
1928	67,1	
1929	83,5	
1930	59,8	
1931	37,4	
1932	25,6	
1933	32,4	
1934	38,8	
1935	40,2	
1936	43,6	
1937	60,7	– Re-armament
1938	46,1	
1939	50,6	
1940	63,6	
1941	62,0	Official control prices (1941–1945)
1942	62,0	
1943	62,0	
1944	62,0	
1945	62,0	
1946	77,2	Official control prices (1946–1952)
1947	130,6	
1948	134,0	
1949	133,0	
1950	179,0	
1951	220,7	
1952	259,5	
1953	256,3	– average of control prices
1954	249,3	London Metal Exchange cash prices (1954–1960)
1955	352,3	
1956	329,1	
1957	219,7	
1958	197,6	
1959	237,8	
1960	246,2	
1961	234⅛	
1962	234⅛	
1963	234⅛	

1964 £ per ton

Jan	14	£235⅛	July	28	£319½
Feb	25	£270	Aug	25	£357
March	24	£255½	Sept	22	£427½
April	21	£318½	Oct	27	£501¼
May	26	£278½	Nov	24	£507½
June	26	£287½	Dec	28	£368

1965 £ per ton

Jan	26	£340½	July	27	£437
Feb	23	£437½	Aug	24	£454
March	23	£477½	Sept	28	£491½
April	27	£490	Oct	26	£518¾
May	28	£481¼	Nov	23	£526
June	22	£450	Dec	21	£550½

1966 £ per ton

Jan	25	£647	July	26	£522½
Feb	22	£676½	Aug	23	£357
March	22	£645½	Sept	27	£428½
April	26	£557½	Oct	25	£460½
May	24	£647½	Nov	22	£459
June	21	£612½	Dec	20	£433¼

1967 £ per ton

Jan	24	£446½	July	25	£373¼
Feb	21	£427¾	Aug	22	£384½
March	20	£396½	Sept	26	£401½
April	25	£345½	Oct	27	£420½
May	16	£375	Nov	21	£558½
June	27	£354¼	Dec	22	£600

1968 £ per ton

Jan	16	£581½	July	23	£446½
Feb	27	£787½	Aug	20	£456½
March	26	£622½	Sept	24	£474¼
April	16	£543	Oct	29	£468¾
May	14	£465¾	Nov	26	£487¼
June	25	£475½	Dec	27	£494½

1969 £ per ton

Jan	14	£527½	July	22	£618
Feb	25	£537½	Aug	19	£685½
March	25	£547¾	Sept	23	£654
April	15	£580	Oct	28	£660
May	13	£584½	Nov	25	£703½
June	24	£623½	Dec	27	£711

1970 £ per ton

Jan	27	£657	July	28	£570¼
Feb	24	£683½	Aug	25	£516¾
March	24	£743	Sept	22	£522¼
April	28	£692½	Oct	20	£456¾
May	26	£612½	Nov	24	£449½
June	23	£603	Dec	29	£437¾

1971 £ per ton

Jan	25	£418	July	27	£448¾
Feb	22	£430½	Aug	24	£449½
March	23	£488	Sept	21	£623¼
April	27	£517	Oct	19	£420¼
May	25	£449¼	Nov	23	£393¼
June	22	£447	Dec	28	£407¾

1972 £ per ton

Jan	25	£412¼	July	25	£420¼
Feb	22	£430¼	Aug	29	£438¾
March	27	£438¼	Sept	26	£429¾
April	25	£426¼	Oct	24	£427¾
May	30	£410½	Nov	28	£426¼
June	27	£415¾	Dec	18	£436

Sources: 1855-1906, *Memoirs of the Geological Survey of England and Wales. The Geology of Falmouth and Truro and of the Mining District of Camborne and Redruth*, by J. B. Hill and D. A. MacAlister, (London, H.M.S.O. 1906), pp. 312-314

1914-1960, F. L. Coleman, *The Northern Rhodesian Copperbelt, 1899-1962*, (Manchester, Manchester University Press 1971), pp. 21, 75 and 145

1961-1972, *The Financial Mail*, (the figures quoted are London Metal Exchange prices)

TABLE C

Table of Companies, 1854-55
From E. Blancheton, *Vade-mecum*
The following corrections to the Table were noted by Blancheton

Column	*Line*	
4	7	Instead of H. Hewitt read H. Hewitt jun.
4	17	Instead of J. Wilson read H. Hewitt sen.
4	18	Instead of P. G. van der Byl read J. Maynier
4	36	Add the name of Mr H. Gordon as Secretary
5	2	Add the names of Messrs G. Kennet & Co., residing in London, as Agents
5	17	Add the names of Messrs G. Kennet & Co., residing in London, as Agents
6	7	Add the figure 8
8	2	Add the number 9 000
8	7	Add the number 120
10	2	Instead of 35 read 75
13	14	Instead of £7 read £10
14	14	Instead of 70 000 read 100 000
16	5	Add the number 8 000
17	5	Add the number 17 000
18	5	Add the number 80 000
19	5	Add £0 2s 6d
20	1	Instead of 1 700, read 6 000
20	4	Instead of 'unknown' read 3 750
20	29	Add the number 2 500

Since the time of completion of the Table a number of companies were formed in addition to the ones enumerated. These were The Ezel's Fontein Mining Company, The New Walwich Bay Mining Company, The Rietberg Mining Company, The Numies Mining Company, and the Koper Kop Mining Company

TABLE D

Memorandum re native labour employed by The Cape Copper Company Limited

Where employed	*Nature of work*	*No. of Natives at present employed*	*No. of Natives that could be employed*	*Pay per day*	*Remarks*
O'okiep, Spectakel and Trial Mines	Underground Drilling and removing the broken mineral	180 men	250 men	2s to 5s	70 labourers could be employed
O'okiep, Spectakel and Trial Mines Dressing-Floors	Breaking, screening, picking, etc.	121 men, boys and women	131	4d to 3s	10 labourers could be employed
O'okiep, Spectakel and Trial Mines Mill-House	Tramming, loading for Stonebreaker, etc.	11 men		2s 6d to 5s	
O'okiep, Spectakel and Trial Mines Washing-Floors	Washing ore	5 men		1s 9d to 3s	
O'okiep, Spectakel and Trial Mines Surface	Sundry duties, such as: receiving and unloading goods, tramming ore, mending bags, etc.	43 men 27 women 5 boys — 75 —		1s to 4s 6d	
O'okiep, Spectakel and Trial Mines Engineers Dept	Stoking, etc.	13 men and boys	16	1s to 7s	3 labourers @ 3s per day could be employed
O'okiep, Spectakel and Trial Mines Surface	Sharpening drills, strikers, etc.	11 men and boys		1s to 7s	
	Tramming refuse	4 men		3s	
O'okiep, Spectakel and Trial Mines Smelting-works	Breaking, piling for burning, filling into trucks, feeding cupolas and sundry labour	64 men and boys	84	1s to 6s	20 labourers @ 2s 6d to 3s 6d per day could be employed
O'okiep, Spectakel and Trial Mines Building Dept	Masons' work, brickmaking, etc.	19 men		1s 6d to 5s 6d	

TABLE D

Memorandum re native labour employed by The Cape Copper Company Limited

Where employed	*Nature of work*	*No. of Natives at present employed*	*No. of Natives that could be employed*	*Pay per day*	*Remarks*
O'okiep, Spectakel and Trial Mines Stables	Grooming, driving, etc.	12 men		3s to 3s 6d	
O'okiep Sanitary Dept	Driving night soil carts and general sanitary work	16 men		2s to 3s 6d	
O'okiep Waterworks	Driving water cart, cleaning tanks, etc.	6 men		2s 6d to 3s 6d	
Port Nolloth	Filling and carrying ore, coal, coke, etc.	50 men	80	2s 6d to 3s	30 labourers wanted
Railway	Maintenance of railway	61 men	67	2s 3d to 3s 9d	6 labourers @ 2s 9d per day could be employed
Railway	Conductors, drivers, leaders, stable overseers, artisans	138		2s 6d to 5s	

(Source: N.A. 212)

TABLE E

Year ended	*Blister copper short tons*	*Dividend per share*	*Dividends*	*% on issued capital*
June 30, 1941	11 000..approx.			
June 30, 1942	11 000..approx.			
June 30, 1943	13 643			
June 30, 1944	13 483			
June 30, 1945	13 903			
June 30, 1946	16 348	1s	£ 51 052 16s 0d	10
June 30, 1947	17 763	3s	153 158 8s 0d	30
June 30, 1948	21 359	9s	459 475 4s 0d	90
June 30, 1949	19 305	14s 3d	727 502 8s 0d	142
June 30, 1950	22 303	8s	408 422 0s 0d	80
June 30, 1951	22 707	29s	1 480 531 0s 0d	290
June 30, 1952	23 622	45s	2 348 429 0s 0d	450
June 30, 1953	24 063	48s	2 450 534 0s 0d	480
June 30, 1954	27 554	46s	2 348 429 0s 0d	460
June 30, 1955	29 428	52s	2 654 746 0s 0d	520
June 30, 1956	32 327	90s	4 594 752 0s 0d	900
June 30, 1957	31 311	75s	3 828 960 0s 0d	750
June 30, 1958	34 859	21s	1 072 109 0s 0d	210
June 30, 1959	38 090	44s	2 246 323 0s 0d	440
June 30, 1960	39 457	60s	3 063 168 0s 0d	600
June 30, 1961	38 909	R 5,00	R 5 105 280,00	500
June 30, 1962	39 654	4,50	4 594 752,00	450
June 30, 1963	40 776	5,00	5 105 280,00	500
June 30, 1964	45 953	5,50	5 615 808,00	550
June 30, 1965	46 077	10,50	10 721 088,00	1 050
June 30, 1966	43 157	14,00	14 294 784,00	1 400
Dec 31, 1966 6 months	21 748	7,00	7 147 392,00	700
Dec 31, 1967	42 529	12,50	12 763 200,00	1 250
Dec 31, 1968	41 441	10,00	10 210 560,00	1 000
Dec 31, 1969	37 399	11,00	11 231 616,00	1 100
Dec 31, 1970	39 517	11,00	11 231 616,00	1 100
Dec 31, 1971	38 021	4,50	4 594 752,00	450
Dec 31, 1972	—	3,75	3 828 960,00	375

Since 1969 copper short tons have been metricated to copper metric tons:
1969 – 33 928
1970 – 35 850
1971 – 34 492
1972 – 36 937

TABLE F

Ore reserves period ended	Metric tons 000s	Short tons 000s	Grade % copper	Copper content Metric tons	Short tons
June 30, 1965	25 552	28 166	1,81	463 516	510 934
June 30, 1966	23 946	26 396	1,81	432 599	476 854
Dec 31, 1967	23 052	25 410	1,73	399 213	440 053
Dec 31, 1968	24 884	27 430	1,62	402 677	443 891
Dec 31, 1969	28 208	31 094	1,60	450 862	496 985
Dec 31, 1970	27 482	30 294	1,54	424 309	467 716
Dec 31, 1971	25 059	27 623	1,55	389 741	429 616
Dec 31, 1972	25 436	—	1,56	397 580	—

Major additions to ore reserves occurred at the existing mines of Carolusberg and Koperberg Central during 1972. No new discoveries were made outside existing ore bodies

TABLE G

Mine production for the year ended December 31, 1972

Mine	*Metric tons*	*Grade %*
Nababeep West	286 900	0,76
Nababeep South	133 110	1,42
Valentine	47 930	1,07
Nababeep Kloof	12 720	0,96
Jan Coetzee	334 080	1,14
East O'okiep	99 390	2,03
Rietberg	622 780	1,39
Wheal Heath	129 820	0,88
Homeep West	67 220	3,15
Homeep.East	1 330	1,04
Carolusberg	771 930	1,36
Koperberg Central	344 510	1,11
Jubilee	295 380	1,25

Jan Coetzee and Nababeep South are nearing exhaustion. Wheal Heath was exhausted during the year

SOURCE LIST

Archival Sources

Cape Archives Depot

Receiver of Land Revenue

R.L.R. 24, *Oude Wildschutte Boek,* April 22, 1775-December 12, 1776

Colonial Office

C.O. 862 Letters received from Sundry Committees, 1866
C.O. 911 Letters received from Sundry Committees, 1869
C.O. 3096 Letters received from Civil Commissioners, M-O, 1866
C.O. 4393 Arrear Correspondence, Departmental, Lieut-Governor, Military and Arrear Memorials, 1852

Native Affairs

N.A. 207 Letters received from Civil Commissioners and Resident Magistrates in the Colony, 1890, 1891, 1892
N.A. 212 Letters received from Civil Commissioners and Resident Magistrates in the Colony. Knysna-Port St. John's, 1892

House of Assembly

H.A. 77 Annexures, 132-250, 1868
H.A. 761 Petitions, 1-78, 1863

Prime Ministers Office

P.M.O. 215 Correspondence from 1906

Springbok Magistracy

1/SBK 5/1/1-5/1/14 Papers despatched by Civil Commissioner-General, Oct 1855-Dec 1895
1/SBK 5/3/1-5/3/19 Papers despatched by the Resident Magistrate and Civil Commissioner to Departments. Jan 1896-Mar 1913
1/SBK 5/4/21-22 Papers despatched by Resident Magistrate and Civil Commissioner, miscellaneous, Nov 1913-July 1914

Accessions

Acc. 612 (34) Willis Papers, Letters Received: Semi-official. May-June 1882
Acc. 1782 (1) 'The Siege and Relief of O'okiep', by H. R. Moffatt
(2) Mrs J. Henwood's siege diary
Acc. 1783 Boer War 1899-1902, Siege of O'okiep, Defence Orders

Government Publications

G.8 – '54, *Correspondence on the Subject of the Discovery of Metals in Namaqualand*
S.C.8 – '54, *Report of the Select Committee appointed to Report upon the Construction of Railways in this Colony*
G.8 – '55, *Reports of the Surveyor-General Charles D. Bell, on the Copper Fields of Little Namaqualand and of Commander M. S. Nolloth, of H.M.S. 'Frolic', on the Bays and Harbours of that Coast*
S.C.2 – '55, *Report of Committee appointed to Inquire into the practicability of Introducing Railway Communication into this Colony*
G.34 – '56, *Report of the Civil Commissioner of Namaqualand on the state of the roads from the mining districts to the ports of export*
G.35 – '56, *Provisional Report &c., by Andrew Wyley*

S.C.5 – '56, *Report from the Select Committee of the House of Assembly on the Petition of Leaseholders of Land in Namaqualand*
G.36 – '57, *Report upon the Mineral and Geological structure of South Namaqualand and the Adjoining Mineral Districts, by Andrew Wyley*
A.97 – '61, *Correspondence on the subject of the Seat of Magistracy of Namaqualand*
A.103 – '61, *Correspondence on the Subject of the Seat of Magistracy of Namaqualand*
A.3 – '63, *Report of the Select Committee on Thefts of Livestock*
S.C.5 – '64, *Report of the Select Committee on the Present System of Leasing the Copper Mines in Namaqualand*
A.7 – '65, *Memorial of certain Miners, Agriculturists, and others of the Division of Namaqualand*
S.C.8 – '65, *Report of the Select Committee appointed to consider Petitions with regard to the Construction of Lines of Main Road from Clanwilliam to Springbok, and on the Bill to authorize The Cape Copper Company to construct a Line of Tramway or Railway between Hondeklip Bay and Riethuis*
Act No. 12 of 1865, Act for fixing the Terms upon which Mineral Lqnds in Namaqualand, the Property of the Crown, may be leased and worked
Act No. 15 of 1865, Act to Authorize The Cape Copper Mining Company (Limited) to construct a Tramway or Railway between Hondeklip Bay and Riethuis
A.41 – '68, *Petition of Matthew Woodifield, Superintendent of The Cape Copper Company (Limited)*
S.C.7 – '69, *Report of the Select Committee on the Port Nolloth Tramway Bill*
Act No. 4 of 1869, Act to Authorize The Cape Copper Mining Company (Limited) to construct a Tramway or Railway between Port Nolloth and Nonams, and to build a Jetty at Port Nolloth
Act No. 3 of 1871, Act to Authorize The Cape Copper Mining Company (Limited) to extend the Line of Tramway or Railway authorized by Act no. 4 of 1869
G.21 – '72, *Report by E. J. Dunn, Esq., on the Country Traversed by the 'Gold Prospecting Expedition' in Namaqualand, &c*
S.C.5 – '73, *Report of the Select Committee on the Namaqualand Railway Extension Bill*
Act No. 24 of 1873, Act to Authorize The Cape Copper Mining Company (Limited) to construct and work a Tramway or Railway from Kookfontein to O'okiep
A.20 – '74, *Correspondence relative to a Line of Railway from Worcester to Beaufort West, &c*
S.C.23 – '77, *Report of the Select Committee appointed to consider and report on the Namaqualand Roads*
S.C.17 – '80, *Report of the Select Committee appointed to consider and report on the Namaqualand Railway*
G.80 – '99, *Report of the Inspector of Mines on the Mining and Production of Coal, Copper, Asbestos and Crocidolite*
S.C.14 – '99, *Report of the Select Committee on Differential Railway Rates*
S.C.7 – '00, *Report of the Select Committee on The Namaqua Copper Company Railway Bill*
Act No. 7 of 1900, Act to Authorize The Namaqua Copper Company, Limited, to construct a Railway
A.27 – '03, *Report of Mr R. Bellechasse Morison on The Cape Copper Company's Line*
A.28 – '03, *Report upon Port Nolloth Improvements by J. M. Searle*
G.11 – '05, *Report of the Commissioners appointed to enquire into Mineral Resources of Namaqualand, with a view to consideration by Government of advisability of taking over Port Nolloth-O'okiep Railway*
A.B.66 – '06, *Bill to Enable the Government to exercise the Powers of Purchase conferred by certain Acts of Parliament*
Cape Hansard 1906
Official Yearbook of the Union of South Africa 1910/16

Cape Blue Books 1856/86
Statistical Register of the Colony of the Cape of Good Hope, 1887/1909
Ann. 647' – 20, *Report of the Labour Registration Officer, Capetown (sic), on the closing down of the Copper Mines of The Cape and Namaqua Copper Companies and the removal in connection therewith of unemployed from these mines*
Annual Reports of the Department of Mines: U.G.34 – '11, U.G.49 – '12, U.G.40 – '13, U.G.30 – '14, U.G.23 – '15, U.G.37 – '16, U.G.40 – '17, U.G.37 – '18, U.G.38 – '19, U.G.50 – '20, U.G.40 – '21, U.G.31 – '22, U.G.27 – '24, U.G.42 – '25, U.G.37 – '26, U.G.30 – '27, U.G.34 – '28, U.G.33 – '29, U.G.21 – '30

British Government Publications
Memoirs of the Geological Survey of England and Wales. The Geology of Falmouth and Truro and of the Mining District of Camborne and Redruth, by J. R. Hill and D. A. MacAlister, (London, H.M.S.O. 1906)

Newspapers
The Cape of Good Hope and Port Natal Shipping and Mercantile Gazette, referred to in the notes as *The Shipping and Mercantile Gazette*, 1846/55
The Cape Monitor, 1853/56
The Cape Mercantile Advertizer, 1854
The South African Commercial Advertizer and Cape Town Mail, 1854
The Spectakel Examiner and Times and Namaqualand General Advertizer, November 1, 1874

Diverse Manuscript Material
Jagger Library, University of Cape Town
E. A. Judge Papers

Library of Parliament
H. R. Moffatt 'The Railway and Transport in Early Namaqualand'

Private Possession of H. R. Moffatt
'Report of the Traffic Manager, N. E. Moffatt

South African Library
J. B. Currey: 'Half a Century in South Africa'

Books
Alexander, J. E. *An Expedition of Discovery into the Interior of Africa*, reprinted Cape Town, C. Struik 1967
J. N. S. Allamand and J. C. Klockner *Nieuwste en Beknopte Beschryving van de Kaap der Goede-Hope; newens een Dag-verhaal van eenen landtogt naar het binnenste van Afrika. Door het land der kleine en groote Namacquas. Gedaan op bevel van wylen WelEdelen en Gestrengen Heer Ryk Tulbagh*, Amsterdam, J. H. Schneider 1778
Ashworth, M. G. *The Life and fortunes of John Pocock of Cape Town, 1814-1876,* Cape Town, College Tutorial Press 1974
Backhouse, J. *Narrative of a Visit to the Mauritius and South Africa*, London, Hamilton Adams & Co. 1844
Journals of Andrew Geddes Bain, trader, explorer, soldier, road engineer and geologist: edited with biographical sketch and footnotes by Margaret Hermina Lister. Cape Town, The Van Riebeeck Society 1949
Barrow, J. *Travels into the Interior of Southern Africa*, London, T. Cadell and W. Davies 1806

Birkby, C. *Thristland Treks*, London, Faber and Faber nd
The Cape of Good Hope Almanac and Annual Register for 1857, Cape Town, van de Sandt de Villiers & Co. 1856
Cape Copper Mining Company Ltd., Report and Accounts, 1876, London, Unwin Bros 1876
Cape Copper Company Ltd., Report and Accounts, 1892, London, Unwin Bros 1892
Cape Copper Company Ltd., Report and Accounts, 1902, London, Unwin Bros 1902
Cape Copper Company Ltd., Report and Accounts, 1904, London, Unwin Bros 1904
Carstens, W. P. *The Structure of Cape Coloured Reserve*, Cape Town, Oxford 1966
Coleman, F. L. *The Northern Rhodesia Copperbelt, 1899-1962*, Manchester, Manchester University Press 1971
Cornell, F. C. *The Glamour of Prospecting: Wanderings of a South African Prospector in search of copper, gold, emeralds and diamonds*, London, T. Fisher Unwin 1920
Cornelissen, A. *Namaqualand Copper History*, privately printed 1965
J. A. de Mist – Memorandum containing recommendations for the form and administration of Government at the Cape of Good Hope: with an English version by Kathleen M. Jeffreys, BA and a preface by S. F. N. Gie, PhD, Cape Town, The Van Riebeeck Society 1920
General Directory of South Africa, 1888, Cape Town, Dennis Edwards 1888
Godée-Molsbergen, E. C. *Reizen in Zuid-Afrika in de Hollandse Tijd*, 's-Gravenhage, Martinus Nijhoff 1916
Hall, J. L. *I Have Reaped My Mealies*, London, Hazell, Watson & Viney 1940
Hanekom, H. T. *Die Gemeente Namakwaland, 1850-1950*, Woodstock, The Nederduitse Gereformeerde Kerkpers 1950
Hawtrey, R. G. *A Century of Bank Rates*, London, Longmans, Green 1938
Heese, J. A. *Onderwys in die Geskiedenis van Namakwaland*, unpublished, PhD thesis, University of Stellenbosch
Holden, W. *History of the Colony of Natal*, London, Heylin 1855
Kotzé, P. W. *Namakwaland 'n Sosiologiese Studie van 'n Geïsoleerde Gemeenskap*, Cape Town, Nasionale Pers 1943
Marais, J. S. *The Cape Coloured People 1652-1937*, London, Longmans, Green 1939
Military Report. Cape Colony, prepared by General Staff, War Office 1908, vol II
Mossop, E. E. *Old Cape Highways*, Cape Town, Maskew Miller nd
The Journals of the Expeditions of the Honourable Ensign Olof Bergh (1682 and 1683) and Isaq Schrijver (1689); transcribed and translated into English and edited with a foreword and footnotes by Dr E. E. Mossop, Cape Town, The Van Riebeeck Society 1931
The Journal of Hendrik Jacob Wikar (1779) with an English translation by A. W. van der Horst; and *The Journals of Jacobus Coetzé Jansz: (1760) and Willem van Reenen (1791)*; with an English translation by Dr E. E. Mossop; edited with an introduction and footnotes by Dr E. E. Mossop, Cape Town, The Van Riebeeck Society 1935
The Journal of Carel Frederick Brink of the journey into Great Namaqualand (1761/2) made by Captain Hendrik Hop and *The Journal of Ensign Johannes Tobias Rhenius (1724)*: transcribed, translated and edited with an introduction, brief lives and footnotes, by Dr E. E. Mossop, Cape Town, The Van Riebeeck Society 1947
Murray, R. W. *South African Reminiscences*, Cape Town, J. C. Juta 1894
Noble, J. *Descriptive Handbook of the Cape Colony its condition and resources*, Cape Town, J. C. Juta 1875
Paterson, W. *A Narrative of Four Journeys into the Country of the Hottentots and Caffraria. In the years 1777, 1778, 1779*, London, J. Johnson 1789
Rosenthal, E. *Other Men's Millions*, Cape Town, H. B. Timmins 1953
Scholtz, P. L. *Die Historiese Ontwikkeling van die Onder-Olifantsrivier 1660-1902, Archives Year Book for South African History, 1966 (2)*, Cape Town, Government Printer 1966

Schumann, C. G. W. *Structural Changes and Business Cycles in South Africa, 1806-1936*, London, P. S. King 1938
Scully, W. C. *Further Reminiscences of a South African Pioneer*, London, Unwin Bros 1913
Simon, J. M. *Bishop for the Hottentots, African Memoirs, 1882-1909*, New York, Benziger 1959
Standard Encyclopaedia of Southern Africa, vol 8, Cape Town, Nasou 1973
Theal, G. M. *Abstract of Debates and Resolutions of the Council of Policy at the Cape from 1651-1687*, Cape Town, Saul Solomon 1881
Theal, G. M. *History of South Africa*, vols III and VII, reprinted Cape Town, C. Struik 1964
Theal, G. M. *Compendium of South African History and Geography*, Lovedale, The Institution Press 1877
Trollope, A. *South Africa*, London, Chapman & Hall 1878
Waterhouse, G. *Simon van der Stel's Journal of his Expedition to Namaqualand, 1685/6;* edited from the manuscript in the Library of Trinity College Dublin, London, Longmans, Green 1932
Williams, A. F. *Some Dreams Come True being a sheaf of stories leading up to the discovery of copper, diamonds and gold in Southern Africa, and of the pioneers who took part in the excitement of those early days*, Cape Town, H. B. Timmins nd
Williams, G. *The Diamond Mines of South Africa, some account of their rise and development*, New York, MacMillan Co. 1902

Articles and Pamphets

Alexander, J. E.: 'Report of an Expedition through the countries of the Great Namaquas, Boschmans, and the Hill Damaras, in South Africa', *Journal of the Royal Geographical Society*, vol VIII 1838
Atherstone, Dr G.: 'Namaqualand and its Mining Prospects', *The Eastern Province Monthly Magazine*, vol II no. 13, 1857
Bain, A. G.: 'Geology of South Africa', *The Eastern Province Monthly Magazine*, vol I no. 8 1857
Blancheton, E.: 'Universal Exhibition (Paris) 1855. Colony of the Cape of Good Hope', *Vade-mecum*, Cape Town, Saul Solomon 1855
Bright, R.: *Lecture on Namaqualand and its Mines*, Cape Town, Saul Solomon 1855
Brumell, G. H.: 'Namaqualand as seen from the Saddle', *New Era*, 22.6.1904
Prospectus of the Cape of Good Hope Copper Mining Company Limited, London, Smith 1862
Chalmers, J. A.: 'Notes on the Namaqualand Copper District' (London, Institution of Mining and Metallurgy, 1900). Reprinted from the *Transactions of the Institution of Mining and Metallurgy*, vol 8, 1899-1900
Cornell, F. C.: 'Prospecting and exploring in Klein Namaqualand', *The State*, vol 6, 1911
Cowie, G.: 'Namaqualand Today', *The South African Railways and Harbours Magazine*, vol 23, 1929
Delesse, M.: 'Notice sur Les Mines de Cuivre du Cap de Bonne Espérance', *Annales des Mines*, 5e série tome VIII, 1855
E.J.D.: 'The Copper Mines of Namaqualand', *Cape Monthly Magazine*, March 1872
Fannin, M. G.: 'The First Attempts at Mining in Namaqualand', *The Mining and Industrial Magazine*, 7.3.1928
Frere, Sir Bartle: 'The Industrial Resources of South Africa'; A lecture delivered to the Society of Arts, 1.2.1881, London, Murray & White 1881
'From Namaqualand to Picketberg Road on Foot', *Cape Monthly Magazine*, October 1880
'From the Sea to the Mines', *The Cape Illustrated Magazine*, vol VII no. 1, Sept 1896

Goodwin, A. J. H.: 'Metal working among the Early Hottentots', *The South African Archeological Bulletin*, 1956
'H.H.': 'The Cape Revisited', *Cape Monthly Magazine*, Aug 1875
'H.H.': 'The Railway from Port Nolloth to O'okiep', *Cape Monthly Magazine*, Sept 1875
'J.S.H.': 'The Copper Mines of Namaqualand', *Cape Monthly Magazine*, July and Aug 1870
Hall, R. T.: 'The Little Railway in Namaqualand', *Cape Monthly Magazine*, April 1871
Letcher, O.: 'Namaqualand: Cradle of Mineral Development in Southern Africa. A series of Articles Constituting an Outline of the History and Development of the Territory and a Survey of its Main Physical Features, Geology and Mineralisation, etc.', *The Mining and Industrial Magazine*, 1932
Macleod, J. M. and Wiid, D. de N.: 'The O'okiep Copper Company in South Africa', *The South African Mining and Engineering Journal*, 20.11.1954
'Nababeep and East O'okiep', *Fortune Magazine*, Jan 1947
Namaqualand Copper 1852-1952, Cape Town, R. Beerman 1952
'O'okiep Copper', *Mine and Quarry Engineering*, July 1964
'O'okiep Copper Co., Ltd.', *Summary of operations in Namaqualand Cape Province*, vol I no. 2
'O'okiep Copper Keeps Growing', *The South African Mining and Engineering Journal*, 20.9.1963
'O'okiep Starts Production', *The South African Mining and Engineering Journal*, 31.8.1940
'The Relief of O'okiep', *The Royal Engineers Journal*, 2.3.1907
Rogers, A. W.: 'An Old Report on the Copper Field of Namaqualand (by F. M. van Werlinckhof, dated 18.3.1686)', *The South African Journal of Science*, 1917
'Stimulating Thoughts in Lusaka', *Metal Bulletin*, no. 5212, 7.7.1967
'The Story of Copper Mining in Namaqualand', *The Mining and Industrial Magazine*, 18.5.1927
Van Heerde, P. en Andere: *Springbok, Die Poskoets – Reëlingskomitee van Springbok*, 1952

Bibliographies consulted

Dowdle, K.: *A Bibliography of Namaqualand*, Cape Town, University School of Librarianship 1955
Robertson, J. K.: *The History of the Narrow Gauge Railways in South Africa*, University of South Africa, Department of Librarianship 1968